PUFFIN  KU-197-559

Edited by Eleanor Graham

PS85

GOING TO A CONCERT

LIONEL SALTER

This is a book for people going to their first big concerts, not quite sure how to understand them, or what to look for in the performance. It is written by a musician of wide experience and reputation, a pianist and conductor, writing from first-hand knowledge of the things you need to know in order to understand and appreciate intelligently what you hear.

He explains how an orchestra is made up, about the instruments used and the different parts each plays, the work of the conductor, the various kinds of music performed, different types of concert, and says something about those who wrote the music. So he helps you to use your whole mind as well as your ears, and to enter into the contribution each musician makes as well as into the whole perform-ance. He has provided a glossary of musical terms, a bibliography, and pronouncing index. Photo-graphs illustrate the text.

Going to a Concert

BY

LIONEL SALTER

PENGUIN BOOKS

Penguin Books Ltd, Harmondsworth, Middlesex

U.S.A.: Penguin Books Inc., 3300 Clipper Mill Road, Baltimore 11, Md
[*Educational Representative:*
D. C. Heath & Co, 285 Columbus Avenue, Boston 16, Mass]

CANADA: Penguin Books (Canada) Ltd, 47 Green Street,
Saint Lambert, Montreal, P.Q.

AUSTRALIA: Penguin Books Pty Ltd, 762 Whitehorse Road,
Mitcham, Victoria

SOUTH AFRICA: Penguin Books (S.A.) Pty Ltd, Gibraltar House,
Regents Road, Sea Point, Cape Town

—

First published 1950
Published by Penguin Books 1954

Made and printed in Great Britain
by Hunt, Barnard & Co., Ltd
Aylesbury
Collogravure plates
by Harrison & Sons Ltd

CONTENTS

PLATES

BETWEEN PAGES 96 AND 97

ILLUSTRATIONS IN THE TEXT

ACKNOWLEDGEMENTS

Plate 1 is reproduced by permission of *Illustrated*; plates 2, 3, and 5 are from *Picture Post Library*; plate 6 is by courtesy of Messrs John Broadwood and Sons; and the remainder of the plates are reproduced by permission of the BBC.

A Word Before We Start

THIS book is called, you will notice, *Going to a Concert*, not *How to Listen to Music* or even *Listening to the Radio and the Gramophone*. This is because actually being present at a concert will give you quite a different impression of music from listening to a 'canned' performance, however perfect. Until you have been to enough concerts to become familiar with what goes on, your imagination cannot fill in the gaps – you can't visualize that particular tense atmosphere of the concert hall during a fine performance, you can't see the way things are done, and often you can't imagine the actual look of the instruments which produce the sounds you hear.

Many people listen to music on the radio who never think of *going* to a concert. To them I can only say that they don't realize what they are missing. What are just disembodied sounds on the air suddenly come to life in the concert room in the most extraordinary way. The trouble involved – if you can call anything so pleasurable a trouble – is more than compensated for by the increased enjoyment you can obtain. And, with the large numbers of special children's concerts now being run in different parts of the country, it is being made very easy to go to hear good music.

Music is what is called an abstract art – that is, it can't be properly described in words; and so people who write about music have a difficult job if they want to give their readers some practical help. This book, which sets out with just that intention, does not attempt to tell you what music is, how it is written down, what is meant by harmony, and so on. If you are interested in music, you probably know something about that already. What we are mainly going to do here is to see what takes place in a concert hall, what instruments are used, what types of concert there are, what kinds of music are performed at each, and who wrote the music. But I expect I shall talk about a lot of other things by the way.

We all have our own tastes in music, and you will almost certainly prefer certain types to others. But try to keep an open mind about all kinds of music, and let your motto be not merely 'I'll try anything once', but 'I'll try anything at least twice'. It is astonishing how one's tastes change and develop, and anybody will tell you that he has often come to like works to which he was at first quite indifferent, or even hostile. The main thing is to listen – really *listen* – to music as much as possible, remembering that the finest art does not necessarily give up its secrets at the first attempt.

I have tried to keep this book as simple as possible, but have not hesitated to bring in useful technical terms where I felt it would be more cumbersome to avoid them: besides, music has its own language just as cricket has, and imagine trying to talk about cricket without using words like 'wicket', 'run', or 'bowler'! Anyway, I hope you will find this book of practical use if you are making, or are about to make, the thrilling experiment of concert-going. Good luck!

LIONEL SALTER

London, 1949

I

The Part We Don't See

If you go to the cinema at all frequently, I'm sure you must have come across one of those films in which, on the spur of the moment, someone gets up and conducts an orchestra in the first performance of his new piano concerto. (It could be a symphony or some other kind of work, but recently it nearly always has been a concerto.) With no preparation other than a smile at the soloist, or, if we are supposed to be impressed with the seriousness of the work, a scowl at the orchestra, the conductor launches forth on a superb performance of his masterpiece. Or a singer may suddenly be called upon to sing something with an orchestra which is somehow conveniently at hand; and you may have been struck by the fact that the mere whisper of the name of the song to the conductor is sufficient for all the members of the orchestra to know instinctively exactly what to play, without such mundane details as being given the music, or being told the key, or anything like that.

But that's in films. Have you in fact ever stopped to consider how much preparation is needed in real life to get an orchestra to perform anything at all? (I mean musical preparation; the business organization is a problem in itself, but this does not concern us here.) You go to an orchestral concert: after the conductor has entered, taken his place on his small platform (or 'rostrum'), and bowed in acknowledgement of the audience's applause, he picks up his baton, and immediately the orchestra plays as one man with all the spirit and feeling the work demands. If you learn an instrument you may perhaps have thought of the pains you must take to make your piece come right and sound musical, and have heaved a sigh of envy to think that these men can sit down and, apparently with little effort, play so beautifully. Perhaps you accept this difference between yourself and them as normal, explaining it away by saying, 'Of course, they're professional musicians. It's their job'. Well, take courage then, if you are one of those hard-working students, because things aren't like that at all.

Let's start at the beginning. A full orchestra consists of anything from about sixty to a hundred players: in the past they were usually men, but nowadays women are taking part more and more in orchestral playing. Now to make so large a number of individual artists sink their personal ideas and play together as a unit is not easy. In your own experience you may have met the difficulties of working as a team with other people, in which case you will know that everybody has his own ideas, but that agreement can be reached most easily if there is someone directing the job – someone in whom every member of the team has complete confidence. If it is hard to obtain a team spirit in most things, it is doubly so in the case of a complicated affair like a piece of orchestral music, one of the most elaborate forms of art in existence, in which the activities of each of those sixty or a hundred people have no meaning except as parts of the whole. Let one of those parts not fit, get out of proportion, or go wrong in any way, and the whole thing is spoilt.

THE MASTER PLAN OF THE MUSIC

The person with the responsible job of directing the efforts of all the orchestral players so as to combine them to produce the best effect is, of course, the conductor. To enable him to do this, he has on his desk in front of him a copy of the music showing everything played by all the different

players – this is known as the orchestral score. It is, if you
like, the master plan, giving every detail of the music, and
the conductor's job is to know this score thoroughly so as
best to control and shape the efforts of his players.

The orchestra of to-day is a complex organization of
about twenty-one different kinds of instruments used in
varying strengths, some singly, some in pairs, and some in
quite large numbers, but in the main they can be divided
into five groups: the woodwinds (instruments made chiefly,
though not exclusively nowadays, of wood, which, to produce the sound, are blown); the brass (also wind instruments); the percussion (drums and other instruments which
are struck); the harp (where stretched strings are plucked
by the fingers); and the stringed instruments, always known
just as 'the strings' (where the sound is produced by setting
stretched strings in vibration either by friction from a bow
or by plucking them). We shall be going into the details of
all these in the next two chapters.

A page of the conductor's score, by which he can follow
what is happening in any part of the orchestra at any
moment, consists of a line of music for each instrument,
these lines being set out one below the other down the page
in an unvarying order – woodwind on top, then the brass,
then percussion and harp, and finally, at the foot of the
page, the strings. You may see what a page of score looks
like if you turn to the illustration on page 25 of this book.

In contrast, the orchestral players, who for the most part
sit in pairs (sharing a copy if they are strings or horns) have
only their own parts in front of them, and have no clue to
what is going on elsewhere. Every so often in the orchestral
parts (and in the conductor's score) there is a reference
letter or number by means of which the orchestra as a whole
can easily find any given place required by the conductor. It
often happens, of course, that some instruments have noth-

ing to do for long stretches (I hope you didn't think that all the orchestra played all the time!) and in that case the players sit counting their rest bars until their next entry. If they have been silent for some time – brass and percussion, in particular, often have very long rests – their parts just before they have to play again will give an indication (called a 'cue') of what some other instrument is playing, so as to make it easier for them to come in again at the right moment. If their re-entry is an important one, it is probable that in addition the conductor will give them a signal to come in.

WHAT THE CONDUCTOR DOES

Let's consider some of the things the conductor has to do. First of all, he must know everything there is to know about all the instruments in the orchestra, their particular qualities, and what they can and cannot do. He must know in each case their good and bad points, the most effective part of each instrument's compass (or 'register') and its most effective styles. He must without conscious thought be able to hear in his head the kind of sounds each will produce in any given passage. He must understand the technique of each instrument, and he should be able to play at least two or three orchestral instruments reasonably well. It is not enough, however, to know about the instruments separately: the conductor must know how they will sound in different combinations – and if you are good at mathematics you can amuse yourself by working out the number of possible permutations and combinations in the orchestra! Merely from looking at the score, he must be able to hear in imagination the sounds represented there, and judge how well or badly balanced they will be. Of course, it helps immensely if he has himself played in an orchestra – by working in the very centre of things it is always possible to learn so very much more than by the keenest outside study – and many conductors have started as orchestral players, most often as string players. Barbirolli and Toscanini were cellists, Basil Cameron, Eugene Ormandy, van Beinum, and Eugene Goossens were violinists, and Hermann Scherchen and Anthony Collins played the viola.

Long before he meets the orchestra, the conductor must become thoroughly intimate with all the details of his scores, so that, when it comes to conducting a work, he knows in advance precisely what to look for and can give all his attention to obtaining the effects he wants. In the well-known phrase, he must have 'the score in his head, not his head in the score'. As a good example of this, there is a story about Toscanini: he was approached in the interval of a concert by one of his double-bass players, who told him his bottom string had snapped and apologized for not having a spare. Toscanini thought hard for a few moments and then said, 'It's quite all right. You don't in fact use that string for more than two notes in the next work, and those two you can play an octave higher in unison with the cellos.' As another example of this superb memory for detail, I have heard the Italian conductor Victor de Sabata at rehearsal telling off a cello section because he remembered (without a score) that a *crescendo* in their part started *one beat* later than they had actually started it!

At the orchestral rehearsals the conductor's familiarity with the score, and his trained ear, will enable him immediately to detect and correct any mistakes of notes, rhythm, or dynamics (that is, the relative loudness of any passage). These may be players' errors or misjudgements, or they may be the result of mistakes actually written in the orchestral parts. I don't wish to exaggerate this particular duty, which any conductor will tell you is the least constructive and the most negative of his tasks, but obviously it is important, and it does demand a highly-trained ear and great concentration from the conductor. I have heard the late Sir Henry Wood, rehearsing for the first performance of a seemingly impossibly complicated modern score, stopping at the climax of a torrent of noise to point out coolly that the second clarinet had played an F natural instead of an F sharp in the previous bar. Sir Henry, or indeed any other conductor worth his salt, would not have considered that there was anything remarkable in his noticing this.

FINER POINTS OF THE CONDUCTOR'S JOB

It is not sufficient merely to ensure accuracy. The conductor next has to see that the balance of sound from the different instruments faithfully reproduces what the composer had in mind. The players in the orchestra are unable to tell if they are producing too little or too much tone in any part of the work, and only someone not himself producing a sound is able to decide upon the right proportions. It may be that an instrument playing a solo passage does not stand out clearly from the accompanying texture. The conductor must judge whether it is the accompaniment which is too loud or the solo which is too soft. The whole effect of the music will be changed according to the way he alters the balance. It may be that the harmony sounds insecure because, of four horns playing a chord, one playing an essential note is too soft for the others; or certain notes may stand out too much from a loud orchestral passage because, for example, the tone of trumpets and trombones is more penetrating than that of other instruments.

The conductor has to judge the proper *tempo* (speed) of the work, and indicate it clearly to the orchestra by movements of his baton. He must be particularly careful to mark each bar as it passes for the benefit of those who are counting rests. But music does not move mechanically. If it did, it would be sufficient to play the orchestra a couple of ticks from a metronome, or, as sometimes in dance bands, say 'One – two', to set the right tempo for the whole piece. One of the beauties of music lies in its subtle variations of pace – the urging on, the yielding, the big broadening. It would be a remarkable body of players indeed who could all feel these subtleties at the same moment and to the same extent; and so, wisely, orchestras decide to give up their individual ideas on pace variations and agree to follow the conductor.

Again, it is up to the conductor to see that the orchestra attacks, and moves, exactly together, and to shape the phrasing (and, in the case of the strings, the bowing) in order to obtain the ideal effect he always has to keep in mind. Shall there be greater or less accent, smoother or more *staccato* playing, larger or smaller differentiations of volume? All these things he must decide, and by keeping an over-all view as well as examining every detail, he must ensure that the work builds up satisfactorily to its proper climax and subsides again, rather than let the orchestra waste its energies in producing a series of unrelated climaxes which spoil the shape of the work as a whole.

Above all this, it must be remembered that orchestral players are not machines but human beings, and, like most people, need someone to inspire them to give of their best all the time. The conductor must therefore know how to handle his players not only so that they are willing to work with him, but so that they will exert every effort to satisfy his demands. He must inspire them with his enthusiasm, guide them through every difficulty, watch every detail, and feel the urge of the music as deeply as they do, yet at the same time he must somehow detach himself from them all and bring his powers of analytical judgement to bear to see that the emotion of the moment is consistent with the larger view of the work which he is trying to express. Finally, though interpretations do of course differ, a conductor, if he is to keep his artistic conscience clear, must resist the temptation to place himself above the music and so make it a mere reflection of his own personality ('my' Beethoven, 'my' Elgar): he must devote his energies to a faithful representation of the composer's intentions.

THE CONDUCTOR AND THE BATON

At orchestral rehearsals the conductor can, and does, explain his wishes verbally, but most of the time, and of course at concerts, he must convey his meaning and lead his players entirely by gesture (and – though the principle is not usually accepted – by facial expression!). It is obvious that a vigorous sweep of the conductor's arm will suggest a more full-blooded tone than a small unemphatic beat. One of the most difficult things to know is exactly which gestures are useful to the orchestra and which are superfluous. This is where it helps to have been an orchestral player first; experience at the receiving end would prevent many conductors from making unnecessary and pointless gestures. Orchestral players are a shrewd lot and very quickly size up a conductor who is new to them. If they respect him they will do anything for him; if they suspect his competence or his sincerity they will mostly ignore him, giving a performance as far as possible off their own bat just good enough not to let down their own reputation. Nothing is more calculated to confuse and annoy an orchestra than a lot of meaningless gesticulation aimed at impressing the audience – 'playing to the gallery'. From the audience's point of view, it is only too easy to be distracted from really listening to the music by the sight of a conductor's gymnastics, but it is a temptation we should resist firmly. This is not to say, however, that we shouldn't note the vigorous style of, say, de Sabata and compare it with the restraint of Boult, for example.

Conductors have not always worked with the kind of stick we see now. The earliest 'conductors' did no more than beat out the time, and one of the earliest mentions of the art (in Rome in the fifteenth century) tells of someone beating time with a roll of paper. This method was quite common, though for some considerable time it was also the custom for the chief performer (who sat at the harpsichord, the predecessor of the piano) to indicate the tempo with his hand, head, or even his foot, while he played. Not all methods were so relatively unobtrusive; in France it was customary to thump on the floor or the music-desk with a stick – in fact, the composer Lully in 1687, beating out the time with a heavy stick on the floor, struck his foot so hard that he developed an abscess from which he died. Another observer in Paris twenty years later wrote that 'the Master of Musick beat Time on a Table put there for that purpose, so loud that he made a greater Noise than the whole Band'. This barbarous habit was still giving rise to protest in France as late as 1767.

Gradually the custom came in of having the orchestra led by the chief violinist, who, in the intervals of playing, waved his bow as a guide to the orchestra. This practice remained for a very long time, and was often a joint effort with that of the harpsichord or piano leader, although early in the nineteenth century, when scores were becoming increasingly complex, a small baton had begun to be used. (Spohr claimed that when in 1820 he started to conduct a concert of the London Philharmonic Society with a baton, people were quite alarmed!) By the middle of the century, the violinist-leader had given way to the conductor in the modern sense. He still keeps a vestige of his former position, however: as the principal violinist of the orchestra (known as the 'leader', or, in America, the 'concert-master'), he sits nearest the audience at the conductor's left hand and is the orchestra's chief representative and spokesman in dealing with managements or conductors. Artistically, too, his advice and technical experience are often called on.

People sometimes ask, 'Is a conductor really necessary? Couldn't an orchestra look after itself?' Well, the experiment of conductorless orchestras was tried, with varying success, in Moscow, New York, and Budapest in the 1920's. It was found that *if* all the members of the orchestra learned the complete score, and *if* a very large number of rehearsals were possible, and *if* the work were not too new or too complicated, the experiment might work reasonably well, but as better results could be obtained more quickly with a conductor, there didn't seem much point in it. It was an interesting idea, but it was rather like making enormous efforts to run a ship without a captain, or a military campaign without a general. All in all, it seemed a clear illustration of W. S. Gilbert's theory that 'When everyone is Somebody, then no one's anybody'.

MAKING UP A CONCERT PROGRAMME

Let us assume now that it has been decided to give an orchestral concert. It may form part of the season's plans for a permanent orchestra with its own conductor (like the Hallé or the City of Birmingham Symphony orchestras), or of a permanent orchestra which chooses a conductor for each concert, or it may be just an isolated concert organized by a promoter who has engaged both orchestra and conductor. This difference is quite important, because it has a lot of bearing on the programme which we are likely to hear. The permanent orchestra with its own conductor is more likely to offer a series of planned and interestingly balanced programmes than either the orchestra which takes various visiting conductors (who naturally want to play their favourite types of music) or the promoter's concert, where most often a 'safe' programme is offered – that is, one likely to make a financial profit.

Of this last type we have, in the last few years, unhappily, seen only too many examples, where hackneyed programmes and star soloists (preferably those with publicity-puffed reputations) are the order of the day. It is a remarkable thing that the public, normally so fascinated by novelty in other fields, should be so ultra-conservative and unadventurous in its musical tastes. It is true that there must always be many who, with all the thrill of explorers in virgin territory, are discovering the familiar classics, but it is hard to see quite why a programme of new works or of lesser-known classics should always get a poor hall. Those people who express their ignorance of music but who, in the silly phrase, 'know what they like', nearly always mean that they like only what they know.

The programme, then, for better or worse, is drawn up. It is usually timed to run for an hour and three-quarters to two hours, with a quarter-hour interval in the middle. (This is as much as most audiences can listen to with proper concentration.) There is no 'typical' programme, but a common plan (which is capable of countless variations) is an overture, a concerto, and a short work or suite, followed after the interval by a symphony. A work which demands unusual instruments or exceptionally large forces is heard less often because of its cost: in nearly all cases the permanent part of an orchestra is of reasonable size and composition, but is augmented as needed with extra players who are engaged

specially for the occasion. If a very large number of 'extras'
is necessary, as for instance in some works by Berlioz,
Richard Strauss, Mahler, Holst, Respighi and others, it
may prove so expensive to hire the players that the concert
will run at a loss. The permanent orchestra can recoup this
loss by balancing this concert with another on more
'popular' lines, or by engaging a celebrated soloist who is a
box-office attraction, but the impresario organizing isolated
concerts is not willingly going to run the risk at all.

REHEARSING A PROGRAMME

The orchestral rehearsals for a concert are arranged in
periods of three hours (with, according to Musicians' Union
regulations, a quarter-hour break). It will depend on the
finances of the organizing body how many rehearsals can be
afforded for a concert; difficult new works may need several
(which is another reason why concert promoters avoid
them), but only too often, in this country, concerts are
given on two rehearsals, or even on only one. Now it is
perfectly obvious that to rehearse a programme of music of
different styles lasting one and three-quarter hours in a two
and three-quarter hour rehearsal period, it is imperative
not only that orchestral players shall be familiar with the
current repertoire and shall be quick at sight-reading music
to them, but that the available time shall be used to the best
advantage, wasting not a moment. (You see now why it is
so essential for the conductor to be a master of his craft?)
Most systematic conductors allot so much rehearsal time to
each work on the programme, so that something at least
can be done on everything, but it may be necessary to devote
most of the rehearsal to one or two works which present
special difficulties and to skim through the rest of the
programme, relying on the orchestra's experience and hop-
ing for the best.

Before the rehearsal proper begins, the entire orchestra tunes up with the greatest care. The tuning note – A – is traditionally given out by the oboe, from whom all the players take their pitch, or, before a piano concerto, by the piano, but some conductors make their orchestras tune to a special tuning-fork (Sir Henry Wood always did this). Orchestras in the Royal Festival Hall, London, and the BBC Orchestra in the studio have the A given by an electrical frequency-generator (which you can hear if you switch on the Third Programme at five minutes to six). Tuning finished, the orchestra turns to the music on its stands – to save precious time, the conductor should have marked all the orchestral parts with any special requirements before-hand – and the rehearsal begins.

Conductors work differently, but the commonest method is to run through a whole movement, or a large section of a movement, before stopping to correct various points. These may be repeated until they are satisfactory, or the conductor, if he has sufficient confidence in his players, may feel that, having explained what he wants, it is safe to leave them. To show his intentions, the conductor will sing phrases and make gestures or explanatory remarks, often while the music is in progress. In rushed rehearsals, there may not be time even to run through all the works once, in which case the orchestra may be taken through just those patches which the conductor knows from experience present difficulties. It cannot be pretended that this is satisfactory, but it is amazing how much ground a good conductor and orchestra can cover in a short time.

Any soloists in the concert will expect to go through their works with the orchestra, and here there is always the possibility of some fun for the orchestral musicians. There may well be some clash of ideas on interpretation between soloist and conductor, which demands the greatest tact for its settlement; 'star' singers in particular are notoriously temperamental. However, if the conductor knows his job he will have rehearsed with the soloist, or discussed the work with him, before the orchestra meets.

It is a fascinating privilege to watch different conductors at work. Some remain calm and unflustered whatever happens: others, more temperamental, will lose their tempers if anything upsets them, and alternately coax and storm at the players if things do not completely satisfy them: others drive the orchestra to distraction by continually stopping for endless talk and unnecessary explanation. A nice story is told of a famous but loquacious Dutch conductor rehearsing Weber's *Oberon* Overture and going over the solo horn's first bar again and again, with long and detailed discussions of the fairy-like effect he wanted. His explanations developed into a lecture, until the exasperated horn-player, despairing of ever getting past the first bar, put down his instrument and said wearily, 'Yes, but do you want it *piano* or *forte*?'

THE AUDIENCE ARRIVES

So, by the time we arrive in the concert hall, most of the real spade-work has already been done. As we sit there in anticipation, the orchestra (neatly dressed now instead of being in casual rehearsal clothes) files on to the platform, the oboe gives his A and everyone tunes up, the leader comes on, receives his round of applause and also tunes to the oboe, and finally the conductor enters and bows his reception of the audience's welcome. He taps his desk for silence and then raises his baton. For us the concert is only just about to begin: for the conductor and the orchestra, this is the climax to all their work – all the part we haven't seen.

The conductor's score: a page of Tchaikovsky's 'Romeo and Juliet'.

2

The Orchestra: Part One

So we have come to an orchestral concert. I hope you arrived in the concert hall in plenty of time, because there are a lot of interesting things to be done before settling down to listen to the music. (In any case, late-coming, which in general is rude to the artists, annoying to other people, and less than fair to one's own enjoyment, is particularly to be guarded against in concert-going, because nearly all concert managements, orchestral and otherwise, do not allow the audience to enter the hall while an item is actually in progress. So if you come late you will find yourself shut outside for that item – and serve you right!) We want to have time to study the programme and get ourselves into the right frame of mind for listening to the various works. But we must also find out exactly what is what on the platform in front of us.

At first sight it looks an incredibly confused scene. The players are tuning up, making astonishing and strangely exciting noises on instruments of all shapes and sizes. Grunts, bellows, and shrill pipings emerge from the general din. Among the hubbub you may be able to hear some players 'limbering-up' on scales and runs, or practising difficult passages in the works they will soon be playing. An orchestra tuning up is like no other sound in the world, and there is an extraordinary fascination in what logically should be an appalling row. The story is told of an Eastern prince who came to Europe and in whose honour an orchestral concert was given: at the end he was asked how he had liked it, and he replied that he would very much like to hear the first piece again. When the orchestra started to repeat the first item, he cried, 'No! I mean the piece before that – the one they were playing before the conductor came on!'

WHERE THE PLAYERS SIT

If we examine more closely the instruments on the platform, we shall see that there is some organization and order behind the apparent confusion. It is obvious that instruments of the same type will be grouped together, but the seating plan of an orchestra is very much the same everywhere, if allowance is made for the different breadths and depths of platforms. This plan has been arrived at by experience as being the best arrangement to allow every instrument to be clearly heard; and of course it is a great help to a conductor to have the same lay-out wherever he happens to be, so that he does not have, for example, the flutes on his left with one orchestra and on his right with another. A conductor is entitled to change the position of the players if he feels like it, but in most cases he leaves the orchestra arranged in the way it is used to.

On page 28 you will see the seating plan adopted by most orchestras to-day. The forefront of the stage is occupied by the strings – violins divided into two groups ('firsts' and 'seconds'), violas, cellos, and double-basses. This is the most important part – the backbone – of the symphony orchestra, and of course it exists also as a separate unit, as the string orchestra. The players, as we have already noticed, sit two to a desk, and by an unwritten law of the orchestra, the left-hand player at any desk turns over the pages, stopping playing, if necessary, to do so. The right-hand player at the front desk of each section is its 'principal': he plays any solo passages which may occur. The principal first violin is the 'leader' of the orchestra.

As you will see from the diagram, the conductor has the first violins on his left, and the second violins next to them. The violas sit directly in front of him, and the cellos at his right hand, facing the first violins. The basses are usually away on the right, somewhere between the violas and cellos, but further away from the conductor. There are many advantages in this plan, one being that the first and second

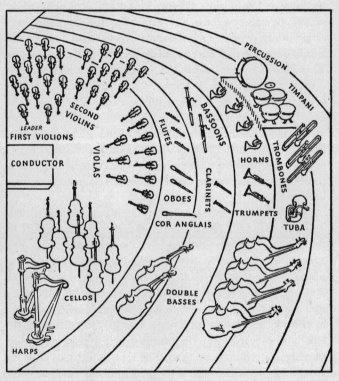

The most usual arrangement of the orchestra.
(See also Plate 1).

violins, who so often have to continue each other's phrases or to play difficult passages in unison, are next to each other and can thus more easily hear what their neighbours are playing. But an alternative string plan is often found. Here the firsts are again on the conductor's left, but the seconds are now opposite them on his right, the violas sit next to the firsts, and the cellos between the violas and the second violins. This method of setting out the orchestra, which is not quite so up-to-date as our first plan, has one extra disadvantage beyond separating too widely the two groups of violins. This is that if the second violins sit on the conductor's right, their instruments are turned away from the audience and their sound is directed into the orchestra: in the first method of seating this is not so, and, as cellos are held differently from violins, they are not subject to the same drawback.

I should add for the sake of completeness that the BBC Symphony Orchestra has recently adopted an entirely new and revolutionary seating position for some of its public concerts; but this is largely because of the problems of microphone placing in certain halls.

HOW ALL STRINGED INSTRUMENTS ARE PLAYED

In all stringed instruments the sound is produced in exactly the same way. Four strings are stretched taut over a bridge on a hollow wooden resonating-box (known as the 'belly' of the instrument), which is pierced by two sound-holes or '*f*-holes' (see page 30). The strings run along the finger-board to the top of the neck, where the tension of each is controlled by screwing or unscrewing a peg, around which it is wound, in order to sharpen or flatten the pitch. The strings are set in vibration either by being plucked by the fingers – this effect is called *pizzicato* – or by friction from a bow, a stick on which horsehair, treated with resin, is stretched.

So far we have four notes, one from each string. Notes other than these 'open' strings, as they are called, are obtained by pressing the fingers of the left hand down on to the string so that only a part of it is left free to vibrate. Remember that the shorter the string, the higher the note. Variations in tone-quality and volume are obtained by different methods of bowing, and special effects can be produced by bowing almost on the bridge (which gives an eerie, squeaky quality), or very far from the bridge, almost on the finger-board (a muffled, breathy tone). It is also possible to touch the string lightly with the left-hand fingers at certain points (corresponding to simple mathematical divisions) to produce what are known as 'harmonics' – strange, fluting sounds.

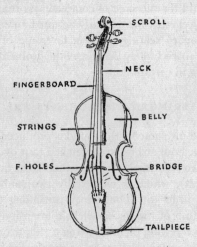

All stringed instruments can be muted by attaching a special gadget to the bridge. The mute makes the tone not only softer, but also woollier and more nasal. Mutes are in common use – except by the double-basses, who seem to scorn them – and are a constant source of irritation to the players, who have not only not to forget to bring them in the first place, but have to find somewhere handy to park them when not in use. The waistcoat pocket is the mute's official home, when the player is a man, but for convenience sake it is very often kept behind the player's ear!

THE ORCHESTRA'S MOST USEFUL INSTRUMENT: THE VIOLIN

In a full symphony orchestra there will be about sixteen first violins and about fourteen seconds. (There is, of course, no difference at all in the actual instruments.) The general appearance of the violin will be familiar to all of you: it is small enough to be held under the chin, as you can see in Plate 8. (To be precise, it is held firmly on the left shoulder not by the chin but by the jawbone.)

The four strings of the violin are tuned to the notes E A D G, as shown below:

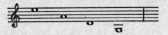

The instrument has a very wide range, from the G of its bottom string upwards for almost four octaves: theoretically, there is no upper limit, but in practice this is as far as orchestral violinists can usefully go. The tone in general is bright and singing, though on its bottom string it is slightly 'plummier', and in the extremely high register rather thin. The violin is perhaps the most useful instrument of the orchestra for any style of playing, from the slowest passages to the most lively and agile, and when the violins as a body play a melody their warm tone is one of the loveliest of sounds.

THE VIOLA: NOT JUST A BIG VIOLIN

Viola players get very annoyed if you say that their instrument (see Plate 9) is a bigger brother of the violin. They hold that the viola must be considered on its own, and not always in comparison with other instruments. If anything, they maintain, the violin is the viola's little brother, for the viola is the oldest member of the violin family, which developed from the earlier viols. The viola is tuned a fifth lower than the violin, which means that of its four strings A D G C, the upper three are the same in pitch as the lower three of the violin; but the tone of the viola is completely different. Instead of the bright, clear tone of the violin, it has a more muffled, melancholy sound, much richer on its lower strings and often rather pinched and nasal in its upper register. The instrument is about three inches longer than the violin, and proportionately wider and heavier. The bow also is shorter and heavier. Because of the great difficulty in getting the left hand round the wide shoulders and thus reaching high up the strings, its upward range is not so great as the violin's. It is safe to reckon just over three octaves from the bottom C string.

If you look at an orchestral score you will see that there is one peculiarity about writing for the viola. Its music is written not in the treble or bass clefs, but in the alto, in which the middle line of the stave is middle C. (The treble clef is used in addition only when the instrument goes up high.) Below you will see the viola's tuning written both in the instrument's own alto clef and then, for comparison, in the treble and bass clefs:

In a full symphony orchestra there will be about twelve violas. It is not easy at first to distinguish them from the violins, but, apart from the difference in size, it may help to remember that generally the viola is held rather flatter than the violin.

YOU CAN'T MISTAKE THE CELLO

Much larger than the violins and violas, the cello (pronounced *chello*) is unmistakable (see Plate 10). It is held between the player's knees and is raised off the floor by means of a spike. The full name of the instrument is violoncello, and if you remember that this means 'little violone' (the violone being the big or bass viol), you will not make the common mistake of thinking of the name as violincello (meaning 'little violin', which is obviously absurd). However, it is too much of a mouthful for it ever to be called anything but 'cello'. Its four strings are tuned an octave below the viola's, and its music is written in the bass clef – except in the high register, when it goes into the tenor clef (in which the second line down is middle C) and, higher still, into the treble. The cello, in fact, has a tremendous compass from bottom C upwards for four octaves.

Its greater size and the length of its strings give the cello a lovely full-blooded tone throughout its range: the bottom strings are extremely rich and fruity, while on its A string the instrument has a glorious singing quality which is unique in the orchestra. The cello has the widest range of volume, from very loud to extremely soft, of all the stringed instruments, and it is useful in all styles, grave and gay. There are usually about ten cellos in the orchestra.

GRANDFATHER OF THE STRINGS: THE DOUBLE-BASS

There is even less difficulty in picking out the basses from the other instruments on the platform. (See Plate 11). The double-bass (sometimes called the bass for short) is so large that the player has to stand up to play it, or sit on a high stool like clerks used to have in old-fashioned offices or like you see in school laboratories. This grandfather of the violin family is tuned differently from the rest of the string group – its open strings are G D A E – and as the notes it produces are so low, its music, for convenience sake, is always written an octave higher than it sounds. Until comparatively recently the bass part in orchestral music tended very largely to double the cello part an octave lower. In the last hundred years, however, there has been a great change in writing for the orchestra, and composers found it a considerable disadvantage that the bass's bottom note should be E, when the cello (working an octave higher) could go right down to C. So some basses were built with an extra string to give them the fuller range; and in big modern orchestras there will nearly always be some five-stringed basses capable of playing low C.

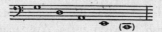

The tone of the bass, as you might expect from so unwieldy an instrument, is thick and elephantine. It sounds gruff low down, and thin and querulous high up: it has to be admitted that, used by itself, the bass can only too easily seem grotesque, but as a foundation for the string group it is admirable. Its *pizzicato* is especially full and satisfying. Like a real grandfather, the bass cannot be too agile or skittish, but it is willing, and will not be left out of a romp if everyone else is having fun. You should see about eight basses in any symphony orchestra.

WHERE TO LOOK FOR THE WOODWIND

So much, then, for the strings of the orchestra. Now let us try to pick out the wind instruments. This isn't so easy, because there are usually only two of each, and as they are much smaller it isn't always possible to see them very clearly. Look for the woodwind more or less directly in front of the conductor, behind the violas – in most halls they are raised above the level of the strings. You will usually find the flutes (and the baby of the flute family known as the piccolo) on the left as you look at the platform, and the oboes next to them. The clarinets and bassoons sit either behind the flutes and oboes (which is most usual) or in the same row.

In the string family there are, as we saw, four different kinds of instrument, and the sound is produced in the same way in all of them. The woodwind family also consists of four types of instrument, but in this case the sounds are produced differently. As a result, the wind instruments have a greater individuality than the strings, and so our ears can easily distinguish between them. You may wonder why there are so few woodwinds in comparison with the large number of strings, but it has been found that, except for works for unusually full orchestra, when more are necessary, the wind players (who are obviously placed far more in the position of soloists than the individual string players) can keep their end up without difficulty.

THE FLUTES ARE BLOWN SIDEWAYS

You will recognize the flutes fairly easily: they are the only instruments in the orchestra to be blown sideways. (See Plate 12.) The flute, one of the oldest of instruments, dates back certainly to Greek and Roman times and probably even earlier, though of course in a much more elementary form than the complicated modern instrument. It wasn't always the 'transverse' (crosswise) flute, either: up to Bach's time we more often find an instrument like the recorder, blown downwards on the same principle as a tin whistle. If you blow across the open end of the cap of your fountain pen, you will get a hooty kind of sound. This is exactly the principle of the flute, except that, being two feet long, it gives a deeper note. As the player lifts his fingers off the holes in the flute (or uncovers other holes by means of metal keys), he is shortening the column of air vibrating in the tube, and thus producing notes of higher pitch. (You remember what we said about the strings – the shorter the string, the higher the note?)

In these days it is fairly common to see flutes made not of wood but of metal, but it is still a 'woodwind' instrument, and its quality remains very much the same – a pure, neutral, rather 'white' or unemotional sound for most of its range, very hollow and breathy in the bottom octave and getting brighter and shriller towards the very top. You can spot a solo flute at the start of Debussy's *L'Après-midi d'un Faune* or of the slow movement of Tchaikovsky's Piano Concerto, or in the *Dance of the Blessed Spirits* in Gluck's opera *Orpheus;* while in the *Dance of the Flutes* in Tchaikovsky's *Nutcracker* Suite there are three flutes gallivanting about together.

There are usually two flutes in the orchestra, but in recent times many composers have called for three. The second (or third) flautist – it's only in America that a player is called a 'flutist' – nearly always 'doubles' on the flute's baby brother, the piccolo. (In the usual happy-go-lucky way that musical instruments seem to be named, the word *piccolo* means only 'little': it is short for the Italian *flauto piccolo*, 'little flute'.) It is played like its big brother, but as it is only half the size it sounds a good deal higher, and to save a lot of ledger lines its part is written an octave lower than it in fact sounds. It is the smallest musical instrument and the highest voice – you might call it the wren of the orchestra. Like all babies, it makes its presence extremely audible – it is bright and piercing and inclined to scream – and it is by temperament naturally gay and lively. You can hear it frisking about in the *Scherzo* of Tchaikovsky's Fourth Symphony.

Very occasionally, as in Ravel's *Daphnis and Chloe*, you will see and hear an extra-large flute in use too; this is called the bass flute, though in reality you'd get a better idea of its scope if you thought of it as an alto instrument, for its range is only a fourth lower than the ordinary flute.

THE DOUBLE-REEDS: THE OBOE GROUP

In the same row as the flutes sit the oboes. It isn't easy to see them very clearly, but they appear to be thin conical tubes played downwards. You can see the details in Plate 13. Like the flutes and all the other woodwinds, the different notes are produced by stopping and unstopping holes in the instrument and thus lengthening or shortening the column of vibrating air. But how is the sound produced in the first place? Look at the picture again. Between the player's lips there are two thin reeds bound together. As he blows, they vibrate against each other and cause a squeak. (Haven't you ever made a squeaker yourself out of a folded privet-leaf or produced a noise from blowing two pages stuck together? It's exactly the same.) There is an excellent opportunity to pick out the sound of the oboe – and it's a very distinctive sound – when the first oboist gives out the A for the orchestra to tune. It's rather thin, very nasal and plaintive, with a characteristic pungent 'edge' on the tone.

The oboe is of considerable antiquity. Its ancestor (called a shawm) was often mentioned in Elizabethan literature, most writers referring to its loud coarse tone. The oboe, when it superseded the shawm towards the end of the seventeenth century, was also loud and coarse, and used mostly for outdoor music; but within the next hundred years it was gradually improved until it became much more subdued and manageable; and now it is capable of the very greatest subtleties of expression. It is the most tiring of the woodwinds to play, for as it must be fed only with a thin but steady stream of air, it calls for great breath-control on the part of the player. The oboe excels equally at long melancholy tunes (like the opening of the slow movements of Schubert's 'Great' C major Symphony or Brahms's Violin Concerto),

BRAHMS: VIOLIN CONCERTO

Adagio

and at gay, pert passages (like the *Scherzo* of Beethoven's *Pastoral* Symphony or in Rossini's overture *The Silken Ladder*).

Beside the oboes sits what is in fact an alto oboe, but is called a cor anglais (English horn) – probably because it is neither a horn nor English! People have tried to explain the name away by saying it ought to be *anglé* (bent), referring to the shape of the mouthpiece (see Plate 13), but that still doesn't explain why it's called a horn when it isn't! But it's important not to think of the English horn as a kind of local variety of the French horn, which we'll be coming to in the next chapter. The cor anglais is a longer instrument than the oboe (it has to be, in order to get the lower pitch), but the principle is the same. The mouthpiece is angled just for convenience, and the bell of the instrument is more bulb-shaped than that of the oboe. Its penetrating tone is akin to the oboe's, but it is richer and deeper, and more sombre: it is best cast for mournful phrases. It is unforgettable in Sibelius's lovely *Swan of Tuonela* or in the slow movements of Franck's Symphony or Dvořák's *New World* Symphony.

COR ANGLAIS
(Sounding a
fifth lower

SINGLE-REED INSTRUMENTS: THE CLARINETS

At first sight, until we look closely, it's easy to confuse the oboes with their neighbours, the clarinets (see Plate 14). They are much the same length, and are played downwards, and they both have lots of metal keys. But a closer examination shows that the instruments are in fact quite distinct. For a start, the mouthpieces are totally different. Instead of the oboe's long thin double reed (the 'squeaker') which we can see vibrating between the player's lips, the clarinet-tist's mouthpiece, which is of ebony, is hidden in his mouth, and, as he blows, a single reed bound to the mouth-piece vibrates against it. This method of tone production causes an altogether smoother, rounder quality than that of the oboe, and once you have heard the two instruments separately I don't think you are likely to mix them up. You can see also that the clarinet has a wider bore, and is cylindrical in shape, not conical like the oboe. The clarinet is very agile, and has a very wide compass: it has great powers of *crescendo* and *diminuendo*, and possesses the useful ability to merge its tone-quality into the general ensemble without drawing attention to itself; yet as a soloist, it has a distinct individuality of its own. However, its voice varies rather as it changes its register: in its lowest part (from almost an octave below middle C) it is very hollow and 'woody': in its middle register it acquires more brightness and produces a full, rich, expressive tone; and as it continues upwards it increases in brightness until it becomes quite strident. The ancestor of the modern clarinet was invented in 1690, but it was Mozart who, eighty years later, started to use it as a regular member of the orchestra, though it had made occasional appearances in orchestral works and in operas before then.

INSTRUMENTS THAT PLAY IN THE WRONG KEY

Before we go any further, there is one matter we should clear up. It is something that puzzles a good many people, but really it is not difficult to understand. Get hold of a score of a work for full orchestra – almost any work will do – and glance down the various instrumental lines. You will notice that the clarinets, horns, and trumpets have a different key signature and appear to be playing in a different key from the rest of the orchestra. That's odd! Yet we know that they *sound* all right, so what does it mean?

The answer is that the clarinets, horns, and trumpets are what are known as 'transposing instruments': they are written in one key and sound in another. This seems extraordinary until we remember that music does not always sound exactly as it is written – we have already seen how the piccolo part is written an octave lower, and the double-bass part an octave higher, than they really sound. In these cases, the players are saved the necessity of reading a lot of ledger lines; but in the case of the other instruments we mentioned, their parts are transposed for convenience not of reading but of playing.

The scale naturally produced on the length of tube which experience has proved to give the best clarinet tone is that of A or B flat, and that means that the easiest keys to play in will be A (or B flat) and the keys most closely related. For although the instrument can produce any note of the chromatic scale, some notes have more awkward fingering than others. And so the clarinet player has two instruments by him, one pitched in A and the other in B flat, and changes about according to the key of the work – or even sometimes of the passage – he is in at the moment. To save clarinettists from having to learn two sets of fingering, one for each instrument, the natural scale is called C, for convenience of writing and fingering, and therefore the written note C for the clarinet 'in A' will *sound* A, and for the clarinet 'in B flat' will *sound* B flat. In other words, and to use technical language for a moment, the clarinet in A sounds a minor third lower than written, and the clarinet in B flat a tone lower. So now, looking back at that score you started from, you will see that the clarinet parts do make sense after all.

By the way, before we go on with the other instruments in the orchestra, we must just go back and mention that the cor anglais always sounds a fifth lower than written (or, if you like, you can think of it as a transposing instrument 'in F') so that it can be played with the same fingering as the oboe.

TWO EXTRA CLARINETS

In the normal orchestra there are, then, two clarinettists (each with his pair of instruments), and you can hear them in unison right at the start of Tchaikovsky's Fifth Symphony.

TWO
CLARINETS
(Sounding a
minor third
lower)

There are also solo clarinet phrases you can easily spot in Weber's *Oberon* Overture and in Prokofiev's *Peter and the Wolf*.

In music of the last hundred years or so, composers have also made use of two other kinds of clarinet, which you may sometimes see although they are not regular members of the orchestra. The bass clarinet, whose compass lies an octave below the ordinary A clarinet, looks something like a kind of wooden saxophone. Its body is of wood, but its curled mouthpiece and its bell (which is turned upwards) are of metal. The bass clarinet's tone is thicker and oilier than that of its smaller counterpart: it reminds one somehow of soft red plush. It is an easy sound to remember. I'm sure you will recognize the gurgle it gives in the *Dance of the Sugarplum Fairy* in the *Nutcracker* Suite – it always reminds me of the last of the bath-water running out.

There exists also a little clarinet, shriller and more blatant in sound, which is used rather less frequently. It appears in Richard Strauss's tone-poem *Till Eulenspiegel* and in Berlioz's *Fantastic* Symphony. It looks just like an ordinary clarinet, except that it is smaller. This rather noisy little fellow is usually pitched in E flat (which means that his written C sounds E flat, a minor third higher). You can see pictures of the clarinet family on Plate 14.

THE BASSOON: DON'T BELIEVE COLERIDGE!

The only woodwind instruments still left are the bassoons, two of which form the bass of the woodwind group (Plate 15). The bassoon is so long that it has to be doubled back on itself, and the tube sticks up above the player's head. It is in fact a member of the oboe family, and so the mouthpiece consists of a double-reed, though it is a little shorter and wider than the oboe's double-reed. Coleridge, in his poem

The Ancient Mariner, talks of 'the loud bassoon', which only
shows that poets prefer imagination to strict accuracy, for
the bassoon is not at all loud. On the contrary, its tone is
inclined to be thin and, particularly in the upper half of its
compass, peevish and querulous – listen for example to its
solo in the second movement of Rimsky-Korsakov's
Scheherazade.

Lower down (and the bassoon descends to a whole tone
below the cello), it is a little fruitier, with a curious dry
quality – perhaps one should say 'nutty' rather than 'fruity'.
When played *staccato* (which suits it well) it sounds rather
grotesque, and as a result the bassoon is sometimes called
the clown of the orchestra; but this is only one of its moods,
and it is equally capable of dignity, pathos, or gaiety. Its
characteristic dry tone is the making of Dukas's humorous
tone poem *The Sorcerer's Apprentice*, while in Tchaikovsky's
Pathetic Symphony it is the very essence of tragedy.

From time to time one sees in the orchestra, as an addition
only for certain works, a ferocious monster pitched an octave
lower than the bassoon – the double-bassoon. Its tube if
stretched out straight would extend sixteen feet, so to make
the instrument manageable it is bent back twice, with the
result that it looks a rather clumsy handful. Its tone is
thick and coarse, and when heard by itself makes one think
of the croak of some prehistoric monster stirring in the
primeval mud: in fact, Ravel in his *Mother Goose* Suite makes
the double-bassoon represent the Beast in the story of *Beauty
and the Beast*. The double-bassoon's detached single notes
can only be called grunts, but the instrument is useful in

adding weight to the orchestra's bottom octave. You can hear it grunting in *The Sorcerer's Apprentice,* in the march section of the last movement of Beethoven's *Choral* Symphony, or in the *March to the Scaffold* in Berlioz's *Fantastic* Symphony.

3

The Orchestra: Part Two

You see that it was just as well we arrived early, for we've been all this time and have still looked at only half the orchestra. Now we must turn our attention to the brass section, who sit near the back of the platform. There are four main types of instrument here, but the number employed of each varies more than in the string or woodwind sections, not only according to the composer's fancy but also according to the period at which the work was written. The four types of instrument are the horns (they are the round curly things with what looks like a forest of tubes), the trumpets and the trombones (both of which you know, I'm sure) and the tuba (the large pompous-looking instrument next to the trombones) – you can see pictures of them all between pages 96 and 97. But before we take a close look at them individually let me tell you about the way they all produce their notes, for it's quite different from anything we've heard about so far, and all the brass instruments work on the same principle. I'm afraid this next section is not going to be very easy reading, but if you really want to understand what you see – and I'm sure you do – you must resist the temptation to skip it.

HOW NOTES ARE MADE ON THE BRASS

The air in a metal tube can be made to vibrate by stretching one's lips across the opening and then blowing, but by changing the pressure of the lips – that is to say, by tautening or slackening them – it is possible to make the tube vibrate not as a whole but in certain proportional parts – in

halves, quarters, etc. The parts in which it can vibrate are
unalterable and are determined by physical laws, and the
whole theory of brass playing is founded on the harmonics
(as they are called) produced by these laws. We have
already come across another use of harmonics in the strings,
you remember, where we saw it was possible to make a
string vibrate in parts instead of as a whole.

Let us assume we have a tube which when it vibrates as a
whole produces bass C – this note is called its 'fundamental':
we will mark this note 1, the harmonic produced by the half-
tube 2, the harmonic produced by a third of the tube 3, and
so on. Then the series will run like this:

(the black notes for harmonics 7, 11, 13, and 14 are out of
tune according to our present system of tuning). No notes in
between those shown are possible. Of course, if we took a
tube giving a different fundamental (a shorter tube giving a
higher, and a longer tube a lower, note), we should get a
different set of notes, but the *proportions* of the series would
remain the same. This is precisely the position that players
of early brass instruments found themselves in: from the
instruments they had they could obtain only the notes of the
harmonic series, and you can see that any kind of connected
scale was out of the question except in the very highest part
of the compass, where the notes of the series fall much
closer to each other.

WHY THE HORN LOOKS SUCH A TANGLE

Horn-players found they could 'cheat' and get a few extra
fake notes by putting a hand into the bell of the instrument,

but this was not very reliable, and the tone of these extra notes was unsatisfactory. So for all practical purposes players were restricted to the natural harmonic series of their instruments; but in order to play in any key the music might be in, they carried, like plumbers, a collection of extra lengths of tube (called 'crooks') which could be added to the instrument, thus changing the fundamental note and thereby enabling them to produce other harmonic series. These crooks were known by the name of the fundamental notes they helped to give: the basic tube of the horn gave the series on F, and players in Beethoven's time had as many as nine crooks which they added as the key of the work demanded. But changing crooks took time, and composers could not put up with so clumsy a procedure and so erratic a scale indefinitely. About a hundred years ago, there appeared an invention which revolutionized everything. A valve system was introduced which did away with all fidgety crook-changing, and made it possible to produce a complete chromatic scale. Various improvements naturally followed, and in the perfected system as we see it to-day, three extra lengths of tubing are welded on to the instrument and, by opening valves, they can be brought into play either singly or together.

That is why the horn (more properly called the French horn) looks such a tangle (see Plate 16). It is coiled round in a circular shape for convenience (for its tube is twelve feet long), and all the 'plumbing' you can see is the valve system, which is controlled by the player's left hand. By pressing down the middle valve, the fundamental note is lowered by a semitone; the first valve lowers it a tone, and the third valve a tone and a half; and as any two, or the three, valves can be combined, you will see that the horn-player has a choice of seven fundamentals and can thus obtain a complete chromatic range instantaneously. The horn used is still that in F, as it gives the best tone, and it is treated as a transposing instrument, the written note C sounding the F a fifth below.

The horns are most useful orchestral instruments. Their tone – round and mellow when played softly, and rich and brilliant when played loudly – blends beautifully with either the woodwind or the brass group, and they form a most convenient link between the two. They have the same facility as the clarinets for sinking out of sight, and they are invaluable for unobtrusively filling out sustained harmonies in the middle register of the orchestra. The number of horns used varies considerably: music by Haydn and Mozart, and early Beethoven works, nearly always ask for two: Beethoven demanded three in his *Eroica* Symphony, and later four. This has remained the standard number up to the present day, though, from Wagner's time onwards, six, eight, or even more horns have been asked for on occasions.

The horn's range extends from the second harmonic up to about the sixteenth (see the example on page 47 again); but as all its notes are produced by the most delicate and subtle variations of lip-pressure (called technically *embouchure*), every player is not expected to cover the whole of this wide range, and the four horns therefore divide up, the first and third taking the higher register and the second and fourth the lower.

You will not be able to mistake the tone of the horn used solo. It has a wonderful passage in the middle of Wagner's *Siegfried Idyll*, and there is a fine short solo near the start of Strauss's *Till Eulenspiegel*. Schubert's 'Great' C major Symphony opens with a solo for two horns in unison. Played softly, the horn can be enchanting – we have only to hear the opening of Weber's *Oberon* Overture, the *Nocturne* from Mendelssohn's *Midsummer Night's Dream*, or the slow movement of Tchaikovsky's Fifth Symphony:

You can hear three horns in harmony in the Trio of the *Scherzo* of either Beethoven's *Eroica* Symphony or Mendelssohn's *Italian* Symphony, while the best examples of four horns together I can think of occur at the beginning of the overture to Humperdinck's *Hänsel and Gretel* or near the start of Weber's *Der Freischütz* Overture.

I should add that a horn can be muted by stuffing its bell with a metal or cardboard stopper or with the hand. Its tone then becomes very muffled and obscure. A special effect can be obtained by blowing a muted horn very loudly, which produces a harsh bray. This 'overblowing', as it is called, is shown in an orchestral score by a small + sign above the note.

THE TRUMPET'S EXUBERANCE MUST BE CURBED

You know what the trumpet looks like (Plate 17), and you know how brilliant and incisive it sounds played *forte*. Unlike the horn, it does not believe in suppressing its individuality, and it is very apt to hog the limelight. This is not to say that the trumpet cannot co-operate, especially in *piano*, but, like a playful tiger-cub, its claws emerge very easily.

Being only half as long as the horn, its register lies an octave higher. All I have said about crooks and valves applies equally to the trumpet, which used to have about

eight crooks but which has now settled down as a fully
chromatic instrument built in two different keys – A and B
flat, like the clarinet – though nowadays the two can be
combined on one instrument. There is another trumpet in
F which is found less frequently, although many musicians
consider it has the finest tone of all.

There are traditionally two trumpets in the orchestra,
though from quite early times composers have on occasion
written for three or four or even more. So many works
written during the last century demand three that many
large orchestras have three regular players as a normal
thing. Trumpets take the upper parts in the brass ensemble,
and excel at agile and brilliant passages. They are particularly good at quick repeated notes, but when it comes to
playing a long connected melody they are distressingly apt
to sound merely blatant and vulgar (as we find in some
scores by Elgar). In Bach's time it was the custom to write
extremely florid parts in the very highest section of the
trumpet's compass (for, valves not having yet been invented,
this was the only part where a continuous scale could be
formed from the natural harmonics), and these Bach parts
can be most exciting, as you can hear in such works as his
Second *Brandenburg Concerto*. Unfortunately the art of playing in this high register seems largely to have disappeared,
and nowadays, with the complete scale provided by the
valves, the trumpet's usual register lies an octave lower.
There is a thrilling solo fanfare (played off-stage) in
Beethoven's *Leonora no. 3* Overture, and you can hear the
trumpets clearly at the start of Berlioz's *Hungarian March* or
Mendelssohn's *Wedding March*.

It is possible to mute a trumpet by inserting a stopper of
metal or cardboard into its bell. This completely changes its
tone-quality, which becomes squeezed and hoarse and, if
the trumpet is played loudly, almost ridiculously tinny and

nasal. But *piano* muted trumpets can be very effective, and not only in toyshop style – they have an unforgettable passage, for example, in Debussy's *Fêtes*:

THREE MUTED
TRUMPETS IN F
(Sounding a
fourth higher)

You may be wondering what, if any, is the difference between the trumpet and the cornet, which is seen a lot in military and brass bands. The cornet has the same range as the trumpet, but its tone is rather blunter and coarser on account of the wider bore of its tube. It is admirable at quick-moving passages, and much better than the trumpet at blending its tone with others, but as a melody instrument it lacks nobility, and more often suggests the public-house than the concert hall. French composers have very frequently used cornets, often in preference to trumpets (although both instruments are used together in Berlioz's *Roman Carnival* Overture and in Elgar's *Cockaigne*), but in this country they are used only occasionally and then as 'extras' in the symphony orchestra.

THE TROMBONE: A VERY ANCIENT INSTRUMENT

The general appearance of the trombone is familiar to us all (Plate 18). I'm sure if you asked anyone to describe it, he would make gestures of pushing and pulling a slide (much in the same way as the request to describe a spiral always results in a corkscrew gesture!). But you may be vague as to what the slide does, and how the whole thing works.

The trombone is a larger member of the trumpet family, and of course has a lower compass. It's a very ancient instrument indeed: the sackbut we read about in the Bible was its direct ancestor. As in all other brass instruments, the only notes the player can produce from the tube by means of variations of his *embouchure* (or lip-pressure) are the notes of the harmonic series; the trombone is the only member of the brass that does not possess a valve system. Instead, it has a slide mechanism which can be extended to produce seven positions. Each successive position lowers the fundamental note (as it lengthens the tube) by a semitone, so that in fact seven harmonic series can be obtained. When you see trombonists pumping their slides up and down, they are changing their basic series with every movement. (Trombones *have* been made with valves, and you occasionally see them abroad, but they are rare.) Now this slide-action of the trombone is important, because it affects considerably the instrument's style of playing. As it has to slide from note to note, the danger is that in *legato* passages, with any but the best players, everything becomes *too* smooth, and phrases become slithery and smeary. It is not very happy with quick *staccato* passages, at which the trumpet excels.

Many musicians (and not merely trombonists, either) agree that the trombone is one of the noblest of all instruments. It ranges from a powerful brilliance in *forte* (for example, in Wagner's *Ride of the Valkyries* or the Prelude to Act 3 of *Lohengrin*) to a wonderfully rich and satisfying sonority in *piano*. One of the most wonderful moments in Brahms's First Symphony occurs when the trombones play in solemn quiet harmony in the last movement:

TWO TENOR
TROMBONES

BASS
TROMBONE

Trombones are not used muted as often as trumpets. In quiet passages muted trombones are capable of producing an extraordinary effect of mystery: played loudly, however, their muted tone sounds more like the bark of a bad-tempered sea-lion.

The trombones are usually employed in a group of three – two tenor instruments and one bass. The bass trombone is larger and deeper than the others, and because of its size needs a lot of breath. (If you get the chance to look at one closely, you will see that the player has to have a handle on his slide in order to reach the furthest positions.) Gluck, and Mozart in the opera *Don Giovanni*, had occasionally used trombones with great effect in operas, but it was not until Beethoven's Fifth Symphony that they made their appearance as normal members of a symphony orchestra: and what a thrill it still gives us to hear them come in for the first time in the last movement!

THE TUBA: AN IMPRESSIVE SIGHT

That leaves only one brass instrument – the big fellow that always sits next to the trombones. It is the tuba (Plate 19), and it acts as the deep bass of the brass group. It is fitted with valves, and its enormous bell is a most impressive sight. For so ponderous an instrument, the tuba is surprisingly mild in tone. It belongs to the horns and not to the trumpet-trombone family, so it lacks their powerful biting edge: its tone may be said to be rather 'tubby' and portly. Its critics say that the tuba does not match up with the tone of the heavy brass: however, its solidity makes up for its lack of aggressiveness, and it manages to get along very well with its more strident neighbours. It is only on rare occasions that the tuba is heard solo, and then mostly for some special effect, as, for instance, in Elgar's *Falstaff*, where it represents Falstaff snoring, or in Stravinsky's *Petrouchka*, where, used in the higher register, it represents a dancing bear lurching about. But the tuba in normal usage can easily be distinguished in the bass line of, for example, Wagner's *Mastersingers* Overture:

'THE KITCHEN'

I wouldn't mind betting that the drums were one of the first things in the orchestra to catch your eye. Most normal people at some time or other secretly long to 'have a whack'. But, like the average boy's ambition to become an engine driver, this doesn't often come off, and in the rare cases when it does it is found that there is a lot more to it than meets the eye.

There are anything from two to five players in the percussion section (disrespectfully but affectionately known to the orchestra as 'the kitchen'), but their chief is always the man who plays the kettle-drums. He cuts a majestic figure with his large drums round him, and, placed as he often is higher than everyone else and in the centre of the row, he appears monarch of all he surveys. His assistants, with an impressive array of instruments to manage, are also worthy of their exalted position. (See Plate 22.)

The timpanist, as the kettle-drummer is called, has three drums, and takes his name from the Italian word for them, *timpani* (remember that it has the accent on the first syllable and that it is definitely wrong to spell it with a *y*, as there is no such letter in the Italian alphabet). Before each work, and often in the middle of a piece, you will see the timpanist bend right down with his face almost on the drums, and then twiddle with taps round the edges. (I was once asked, 'Why does he *smell* the drums so often?') Each of the three drums can be tuned to a note within a range of about a fifth, and as they are of different sizes, the timpanist can play three notes. To tune a drum, he turns a set of screws round the rim, which tightens or slackens the stretched skin. As it is essential that a drum should be properly in tune – not at all an easy thing to achieve – the player taps the parchment lightly, with his ear very close to it. It takes even first-rate players a little time to change the tuning of a drum, and modern composers, who sometimes demand very frequent changes of tuning, have been indirectly responsible for the invention of what are called 'pedal-timpani'. With these, instead of the fussy turning of screws, all the player has to do to tighten the metal hoop which controls the tension of the skin is to push down a foot-pedal. This can be done almost instantaneously, but timpanists are not agreed that the new instrument's tone is as good as that of the old type.

The drumsticks have felt heads, and most drummers have two or three pairs of different degrees of hardness to produce different kinds of tone. Wooden heads are sometimes used for special effects. Don't run away with the idea that the drums, or any of the percussion section, exist only to make a noise. Continuous loud playing very quickly becomes wearisome to the listener, and some of the best percussion effects are quiet ones. Timpani can be played at anything from *ppp* to *fff*: they can execute rolls, single notes, or any kind of rhythms. If you have ever heard Beethoven's Violin Concerto, you will remember the four quiet drum taps which start the work off; and soft rolls can be heard in almost any piece. Loud solo rhythmic figures are often used for comic or grotesque effects, as in the Scherzos of Beethoven's Ninth Symphony, Sibelius's First Symphony, or the Symphony by Walton, or in the tumultuous *Troyte* movement in Elgar's *Enigma* Variations:

A few composers have tried the experiment of using two sets of timpani together, and very successful it has proved, both for mysterious rolled chords, as in Berlioz's *Fantastic* Symphony, and for dramatic climaxes, as in the finale of Walton's Symphony. (If ever you get the chance to hear Berlioz's *Requiem Mass* – and unfortunately it's very rare – don't miss it, if only for the sake of hearing twelve timpanists playing chords.)

A VARIETY OF THINGS TO BEAT

The rest of the percussion instruments (Plate 20) have relatively little to do, and so two or three players move about from one to the other, fitting in anything that occurs in the music. It is only on rare occasions, and then in modern music, that the percussion section is used all by itself, but 'outings' do occur, as, for instance, in Britten's *Variations on a Theme by Purcell* (*Young Person's Guide to the Orchestra*) and in Kodály's *Háry János* Suite; and it is never difficult to hear most of the 'extra' percussion instruments at any time when they do play.

Here are some of them: these have no definite pitch. The *side-drum* (very like the kind you see in a street parade) is small and flat and played with two wooden sticks. It has two parchment 'heads' or surfaces, across the lower of which are stretched wire strings ('snares') which vibrate when the upper head is struck. The side-drum is useful either for stressing rhythms or for rolls, both soft and loud, and its crisp crackly tone can make itself heard even in orchestral climaxes. The *bass-drum* stands upright on its side, and its single head is struck with a large felt-headed stick. It produces a dull booming thud, and I'm sure it's what a crime-novelist would call a 'blunt instrument'.

The *cymbals* are two thin brass plates which are clashed together. Played softly they sound mysterious, and played loudly they can provide that final touch of excitement at the height of a climax. A special effect can be obtained by hanging up one cymbal and playing a roll on it with timpani sticks, which gives a chilling feeling of mounting tension and suspense. In music of Spanish character the *tambourine* is often used. This has a small parchment head and is hung with tiny metal plates which jingle as the head is struck or the tambourine is shaken. The *castanets*, which consist of two small hollowed-out pieces of wood clicked together, are also used to give Spanish atmosphere. The *wood-block* is what its name suggests, and when tapped with a side-drum stick gives a dry, hollow sound. It has associations with the music-hall which are exploited by Walton when he uses it solo in the *Popular Song* of his *Façade* Suite. The *triangle*, of bent steel, is in fact an incomplete triangle. It is hung up and struck with a special steel beater. It should give a light silvery tone, but many instruments in use to-day either give so pure a note that they have definite pitch, or, at the other extreme, sound like a fire alarm. Almost the only composer ever to have used the triangle as a solo instrument is Liszt, in his First Piano Concerto, and to this day the entry sounds slightly silly.

A very large number of people (including many who should know better, such as composers and writers on music) speak of the *gong* and the *tam-tam* as one and the same thing. They are both circular sheets of metal struck with soft beaters, and they have the same tone-quality, but the tam-tam has no definite pitch, giving a rich crash (or an ominous shudder if struck gently), while the gong gives a clear note. Puccini uses tuned gongs with wonderful effect in his opera *Turandot:* the tam-tam contributes one note to the finales of Tchaikovsky's Sixth (*Pathetic*) Symphony and of Rimsky-Korsakov's *Scheherazade*, though you will probably be so carried away at the climax that you'll forget to listen for it!

There are also some tuned instruments played by the versatile percussion players, though of course, like many of those already mentioned, they make occasional, and not regular, appearances in musical works. You all know the *tubular bells* by sight – a row of metal tubes of different lengths hung in a wooden frame and struck with wooden hammers. They give rather an unconvincing imitation of bells, and always seem to be slightly out of tune: no one loves them. The *glockenspiel* consists of a row of small steel plates laid on a flat frame and played with two hammers. Its silvery carillon can pick out and light up the top octave of the orchestra in a lovely, sparkling way. Very similar, but with hard wooden bars instead of steel, is the *xylophone*. It gives a brittle sound which makes one think of dry bones; in fact Saint-Saëns used it with something very like that in mind in his *Danse Macabre*.

All kinds of other extraordinary noises are asked for at odd times by composers: cowbells, tom-toms, anvils (an imitation, not an importation, of the blacksmith's tool), whips, rattles (the football-match type), slapsticks (two pieces of thin wood cracked together – you may have seen them in Harlequinades), machines for imitating wind (in Strauss's *Don Quixote*), and even typewriters, chains, klaxon horns, sirens, and revolvers! These are not taken very seriously by most people, and are generally referred to by the players as 'comics'.

THE HARPIST'S DIFFICULT JOB

I should hate to be a harpist: not only is the instrument a perpetual nuisance to move from place to place, but any harpist will tell you that she (it usually is a she) spends as much time tuning it and mending strings as playing it. She always has to be first on to the platform, long before any of the rest of the orchestra, tuning her harp, and the instrument will certainly need attention again by the interval of the concert. Nevertheless, and despite its difficulty, there *are* harpists, one to a medium-sized orchestra, two to a large one.

The harp dates back to antiquity, but the instrument as we now know it, the so-called Double-Action Harp (see Plate 21), came into being only at the start of last century. By 1830 Berlioz was using two in his *Fantastic* Symphony, and twenty-five years later Wagner was calling for six in his opera-cycle *The Ring*!

The strings of the harp are tuned to the scale of C flat major (running through seven octaves). The player has the shorter strings (the higher notes) nearer her. At the foot of the instrument are seven pedals, each of which acts on all the notes of the same name. That is to say, one pedal controls all the C's, another all the D's, and so on. There are two notches into which each pedal can be pushed: the pedal in the first notch raises all its notes by a semitone (thus making all the notes naturals), in the second by a tone (making them sharps). So, if you wanted to play, say, both C and C sharp together, it could be done only by having your C pedal in the first notch (giving C natural) and your D pedal right up (giving D flat = C sharp), or, alternatively, by having your B and C pedals in the second notch (giving B sharp = C natural and C sharp). I'll leave you to work that out slowly!

The harp's usual type of part consists of arpeggios or spread chords, as in the introduction to the *Flower Waltz* in Tchaikovsky's *Nutcracker* Suite, but isolated notes are often very effective, especially when they are harmonics (for lovely luminous sounds an octave higher can be obtained by making the strings vibrate in halves). A thrilling effect, which unfortunately is grossly overworked, is the harp's *glissando*, where a finger is run across all the strings, which are 'set' in advance to form a certain chord or scale. You can hear this in many works, but a good example occurs in Rimsky-Korsakov's *Spanish Caprice*.

'OCCASIONALS' IN THE ORCHESTRA

That really does seem to be all the orchestra accounted for – but no! there's something that looks vaguely like a miniature upright piano very near the conductor. It doesn't play in the majority of works, and when it does appear it doesn't seem to do a great deal, but if you can spot it in action, you will hear a pleasant tinkly sound that could be described as the musical equivalent of fairy lights. This is the celesta, a keyboard instrument in which hammers strike on steel plates. It was invented in 1886, and Tchaikovsky was one of the first to lose his heart to it, giving it the well-known solo in the *Dance of the Sugar-plum Fairy* in the *Nutcracker* Suite.

Occasionally, in modern works, the piano itself is used as a member of the orchestra, and not merely as a solo instrument. (The violins always hate this, because it involves their being squashed back. They have to put a good face on it in the case of a concerto, but they're usually uncomfortably crowded all the same. By the way, in a piano concerto the conductor sometimes works from behind the piano. This may be due either to modesty or to the fact that with the piano lid open it's difficult for all the orchestra to see him.) Orchestral works with piano passages include Stravinsky's *Petrouchka*, Holst's *Planets*, and the First Symphony by the Soviet composer Shostakovitch, while in Debussy's *Printemps* (*Spring*) there is a part for piano duet. There is another use for the piano, too, in early eighteenth-century music. At this period it was the custom for the harpsichord to fill up the inner harmony throughout a work, and even at certain points for the composer to write out in full only the treble and bass parts and leave the harpsichord to carry all the harmony. This kind of keyboard part, called a *continuo*, is nowadays mostly played on the piano, though only too often the part is left out altogether owing to carelessness or to ignorance of the correct method of playing works by Bach and his contemporaries.

Composers sometimes write a part for the organ. Saint-Saëns did so in his Third Symphony, and Elgar and Strauss, to name only two others, have written organ parts in their scores, but this is a chancy business, because all organs differ greatly in tone, and anyway, not every concert hall has a suitable instrument. What's more, most musicians agree that the organ and the orchestra sound horrible together;

their tone-qualities don't blend, and the organ, lacking the clarity of speech of orchestral instruments, only muddies up the texture.

NOT ALL AT ONCE, PLEASE

There is no limit to the instruments that *can* be included in the orchestra (I've mentioned some of the more extraordinary percussion instruments already) but you may also on occasion come across a guitar, a mandolin, or a saxophone. One very lovely effect sometimes included by composers is a choir of human voices singing wordlessly. Delius uses voices as instruments in this way in *A Song of the High Hills*, while a female choir is used by Debussy to represent the voices of the Sirens in *Nocturnes*, and by Holst in *The Planets* to suggest the furthest conceivable reaches of space. I shall have more to say about choruses in a later chapter.

In order to cover as much ground as possible, I've talked about more instruments than you will see on the platform every time you go to a concert; so don't say, 'I went to a concert the other day, and lots of the things you mentioned weren't there'. I know; but one of the things which used to fascinate me when I first went to concerts was the way all the 'extras' who play perhaps in only one item come on the stage just for that one item and no more. I used to think they didn't want to sit and listen to the rest of the concert, but I found later that the presence of a lot of unwanted players is extremely distracting to the conductor.

Well, we have identified all the instruments on the platform by appearance. What I can't tell you in this book – and what is far more important – is exactly how they sound, and that part of the identification you must learn for yourself by experience. Special concerts for children, which are run by many towns, are a great help; the conductor often makes a point of letting the audience hear the instruments separately first. Concentrate on the sound of any particular instrument you are looking at for the moment; you will be surprised to find how riveting your attention in this way seems to bring the instrument into focus. The orchestra is a wonderful body. After you've been to one orchestral concert I'm sure you won't be satisfied until you can go to others, and you'll find that with experience all the seeming difficulties of the instruments vanish completely.

4

What We Are Going to Hear

BEFORE the concert starts, there is another job we have to
do, and this no matter whether it is an orchestral concert, a
song recital, or any other kind of programme: we must get
ourselves into the right frame of mind for listening to what
is coming. We shall approach a work lasting three minutes
and a work lasting thirty in quite different ways, and we
want to know beforehand what to expect. The programme
will give the work's title, possibly the key and usually an 'op.
number' – for example, 'Chopin: Study in G flat op. 10
no. 5'. The 'op.' stands for *opus* (Latin for 'work'), and this
numbering is merely a means of identifying a work. Thus in
the Chopin example it serves to distinguish that Study from
another Study in G flat, op. 25 no. 9. An opus number
should also give some idea of whereabouts the work comes
in the composer's output, but unfortunately in certain composers' works the number doesn't follow the order of composition but that of publication.

Our listening will be made a lot easier if we know in
advance the plan which the composer had in mind when
writing, for a work of art can never be said, like Topsy, to
have 'just growed'. A composer does not start blindly from
an idea and then turn round at the end and say, 'Bless me!
I've written a symphony'. From the beginning he has to
have a clear idea of what the structure will be.

PICTURE AND STORY MUSIC

Now the easiest music to follow, and in some ways the easiest
to construct, is that which tells a story of some kind (this is

called 'programme music') or which illustrates a picture. There are some people who seem unable to listen to any music without making up some kind of story or seeing some mental picture. I am sure these people would be much surprised and hurt if they were told that this was an un-musical way of listening; but it is so, for instead of accepting what the composer is saying in musical terms, they are tak-ing it upon themselves to invent little stories or pictures which have nothing to do with the music and which only cheapen it. Music, said the poet Goethe, begins where words leave off; so that to make all music tell a story or paint a picture is as wrong a use as wearing evening dress to play football.

If a composer intends people to visualize a picture or story he says so by giving his work a title which makes his purpose clear. But even then it is impossible to say *exactly* what is meant by any particular passage in the music, for music is a language which can suggest moods or emotions but can rarely depict an actual event. So when Tchaikovsky writes a work on *Romeo and Juliet* or Rimsky-Korsakov on *A Thousand and One Nights* (*Scheherazade*), though in general he may be illustrating a story we can never be *quite* sure what any part of the music stands for. Certain works do contain crude imitations of actual events – the breaking of a storm, with its thunder and lightning, the baa-ing of sheep, the firing of cannon, and so on – but it can safely be said that such things are nearly always of smaller musical value.

Much more poetic is what has been called 'suggestive' or 'impressionist' music – Mendelssohn's *Fingal's Cave* or Debussy's *Gardens in the Rain*, for example – where the com-poser has aimed only at giving a general impression of a pictorial subject. One great weakness, however, about all programme music is that, if the title is not given, the same piece may suggest totally different things to different people. And in certain cases, as for example in Debussy's *Preludes* or Schumann's *Scenes of Childhood*, the programme titles were actually added after the music was written!

WORKS THAT STAND ON THEIR OWN FEET

Works without a programme – what is called 'abstract music' – having no story to rely on, have to be constructed, and listened to, in terms of music only. Now if you've ever tried your hand at writing a piece of music you will know that it's quite easy to think of a tune or theme: the difficulty comes in knowing what to do with it. To go on repeating it, perhaps with small variations, is rather like a child building up a tower of bricks one on top of the other: after a certain point the repetition can be carried no further, and the whole structure collapses. So a composer writes according to a more or less fixed plan; one can scarcely call it a 'blue-print' for, as his inspiration moves him, he may decide to modify the plan as it is in progress.

As music has developed, various forms have been arrived at by experience as providing a solid basis on which to build a musical work, and most music you hear will follow, in essentials at least, one of the accepted patterns. In this chapter, we are going to see how some of these forms are made up. Remember always that the form is only the skeleton of the work. Without a good skeleton a work will be flabby and shapeless, but the beauty of the work will depend on the flesh which covers the skeleton and on the way it is clothed. The essence of the problem of form is to find a design which will produce a well-proportioned work with sufficient contrasts and with a suitable climax. I need scarcely emphasize that, besides a well-designed ground plan, the material involved – the themes themselves – must be interesting enough to build with, and strong enough to bear the weight of development.

THE SONATA-FORM: CONTRAST AND BALANCE

At most orchestral concerts you will hear at least one symphony. At most instrumental recitals you will hear at least one sonata. Had you realized that symphonies and sonatas, and most works for small ensembles such as trios, string quartets, and so on, are all basically in the same form? They all normally have four movements: a first movement, designed according to a special plan of its own called 'sonata-form', a slow movement, a third movement (which changed in Beethoven's hands from a Minuet and Trio to a Scherzo and Trio) and a finale – usually gay and often a Rondo. Now in that one sentence I've used several terms which you may not know. Let's turn back and look at them one by one, for we shall constantly be meeting them.

Sonata-form is one of the most common and important forms in the whole of music. It depends on two basic principles, contrast and balance. In the first section of the movement, known as the *Exposition*, two themes (or 'subjects') contrasted in character and mood are introduced and 'settled in'. (Up to about the middle of last century that section was railed off, as it were, by a dividing cadence.) Then the two subjects, either as a whole or in fragments, are played about with, or new material may be introduced to throw the original subjects into greater relief, entirely as the composer's fancy takes him. This section is called the *Development*, and it leads to the third and final part (the *Recapitulation*), in which the material of the first section is re-presented so as to round off the movement with suitable finality: there is sometimes a *Coda* or tail-piece.

One of the ways composers keep up the interest in an

extended movement is by judicious changes of key ('modulations') which will balance one another and strengthen the fundamental key of the work. As after even the most delightful holiday one is glad to get home, so there is a definite musical satisfaction in returning safely to the home, or 'tonic', key. In sonata-form, as in most other forms, this key-relationship is very important: in the orthodox design the first and second subjects appear in the exposition in contrasting keys, and in the recapitulation in one and the same key.

WHAT YOU CAN DO WITH A THEME

One of the most obvious devices of construction is to write a set of variations on a theme. This can form a complete work by itself, but it is sometimes found as one of the movements of a sonata or trio, quartet, quintet, etc. (which are sonatas in all but name) or, less often, of a symphony. A great deal of technical skill is often lavished on the writing of variations, and it may be interesting to consider what can be done with a theme. The variations by earlier masters often consisted merely of increasingly fast and complicated decorations on the melody. (Handel's set nicknamed *The Harmonious Blacksmith* in his E major Suite is a typical example.) By Beethoven's time this had given way to another style altogether. Here not only might different rhythmic or melodic patterns on the same harmony be used, or the theme re-harmonized, or major transformed into minor, but the theme would be developed instead of decorated. A phrase might be extended, or repeated at a different pitch (this was called 'sequence') or an entirely new variation might be built on a single rhythmic, melodic, or harmonic fragment derived from the theme. The character might be altered entirely by a change of tempo (a funeral march variation of a gay theme, for example), or the theme might be cast in the rhythm of a dance-form, or treated with some voices or parts imitating others.

In the case of variations forming separate works (as in the Brahms set on a Handel theme, for piano, or the Mozart-Reger or Purcell-Britten sets for orchestra, or the Dohnányi *Variations on a Nursery Tune* for piano and orchestra) it is quite common for them to culminate in a Fugue (we'll see later exactly what that is). When used orchestrally for the slow movement of a symphony – as in Haydn's *Surprise* (G major) or *Drumroll* (E flat) Symphonies, or in Beethoven's Ninth Symphony – they are always connected by linking material instead of remaining in separate sections.

Another kind of variation form is founded on what is known as a *ground bass*. Here the first short phrase in the bass is repeated over and over, while above it are built changing harmonies and different melodic phrases. The ground bass was used extensively in the seventeenth and eighteenth centuries, notably by Purcell (in a large number of works, including his *Evening Hymn*, and *When I am Laid in Earth* from the opera *Dido and Aeneas*) and Bach (as in the *Crucifixus* of his *Mass in B minor*). It was also taken up by Brahms, who in the finale of his *Variations on a theme of Haydn* produced a magnificent example. You may be thinking that it must sound boring to repeat a short phrase continuously, but the beauty of the ground bass, properly handled, is that one is so interested in the material above that one scarcely notices the repetitions, and in the hands of a master it can be a most expressive and satisfying form. From the ground bass are also derived the *Chaconne* and the *Passacaglia*, each of which was originally a dance but is now somewhat solemn in character; the only difference between them is that the Chaconne is supposed to keep the repeated phrase (called an *ostinato*) strictly in the bass, while in the Passacaglia it can move about into any voice, and can be varied at will. The finale of Brahms's Fourth Symphony is a fine example of a Passacaglia, although it is not actually labelled one in the score.

OTHER MOVEMENTS OF THE SYMPHONY

One of the simplest designs used in music, which you can think of, if you like, as 'sandwich' form, has an opening section followed by a contrasting section, after which the first part is repeated. This, you can see, is an easy way of securing balance while at the same time avoiding monotony. The ear welcomes the new material of the middle section and then accepts gratefully the return of the first section, which it has already heard. This three-section form (the technical name is 'ternary') is very frequently found in works of all kinds. In eighteenth-century operas, the arias or songs were nearly all shaped like this (an example is Handel's *Where'er you walk*), and composers saved themselves the trouble of writing out the first part again by simply putting the letters D.C. (*Da Capo* – from the beginning) at the end of the middle bit, and indicating by the word *Fine* (End) where to stop. The third movement of sonatas and symphonies is traditionally cast in this ternary form, either as a Minuet and Trio or as a Scherzo (literally, a 'joke') and Trio. The Minuet, of course, was originally a dance form, consisting of two parts, each repeated. The contrasting Trio then followed (in Haydn's symphonies this was often made the opportunity for some novel touch of instrumentation); this also was in two parts, each of which was repeated; and then the Minuet was played again, this time without repeats. From Beethoven's time the Minuet was discarded in favour of the livelier Scherzo, but the shape remained much the same, although in Beethoven's later works the Trio sometimes appears twice – what you might call a double-decker sandwich. Later symphonists, including Schubert, Bruckner, and Sibelius, have stuck to the ternary form, but Brahms treated it with greater freedom, and some composers have adopted first-movement sonata-form for their Scherzos.

A modified ternary or 'aria' form is often used for the slow movement also (this comes before the Minuet or Scherzo, you remember). Here sonata-form at a slow tempo would be altogether too long and cumbersome. Ternary form is much less set in the case of slow movements: there are no square-cut phrases to be repeated. Instead, composers have inclined to a freely-developed movement in which the contrasting middle episode leads, not to an exact repetition of the first section, but to a re-working of its material (perhaps compressed). The end of the movement is rounded off with a *coda* or tailpiece.

ROUNDING OFF THE SYMPHONY: THE FINALE

We have touched on all the movements of the sonata or symphony now except the finale. In the last movement, where the difficulty is to provide a suitable and effective finish to the whole work, classical composers (by which we mean roughly those up to Beethoven) usually ended on a note of gaiety, employing the Rondo form. In the Rondo the first theme frequently reappears, with different interludes, usually in other keys: there is often also a short *coda*. If you like to call the main theme A, and the various ensuing episodes B, C, etc., then the whole Rondo will be ABACA (DA. etc., if desired). To avoid monotony, the repetitions of the opening theme may be shortened or decorated. From Beethoven's time symphonic finales have tended to be more dignified in style, providing a climax rather than a happy ending to the work. For this, composers have used mostly either sonata-form (as in the first movement) or a cross between that and rondo form, known as Rondo-Sonata, where the shape could be expressed ABACABA, the B in this case becoming almost a second subject, and, as in sonata-form, appearing first in a contrasting key and later in the tonic or home key.

In the programme notes at a concert, you may sometimes find a symphony referred to as being in 'cyclic' form. (When you do I'm willing to bet that you're going to hear either the Franck or the Berlioz symphonies – it's one of the programme-note-writers' pet phrases about them!) All that 'cyclic' form means is that themes from one movement are used also in the rest of the work; this helps to give some feeling of unity.

WHAT A PROGRAMME NOTE SHOULD TELL YOU

Incidentally, this may be a good moment to say something about programme notes generally. They vary between being very good and helpful and very dry and confusing. Unfortunately the standard is not very high at present, though it is improving. A good note should give us the historical background of the work, tell us something of its importance in the repertoire, and help us – in not *too* great detail – to follow the course of the music. I say not too great detail because something should be left to our observation and imagination: reading a note should never be allowed to take the place of listening and concentrating on the music. Above all things, *do not* attempt to read while the music is in progress, feverishly trying to identify a theme here or a passage there which the writer mentions. It's as fatal as trying to read a map while actually driving a car.

ANCESTORS OF THE SYMPHONY

All musical forms develop and change in use, and the four-movement sonata and symphony have sprung from earlier types. Among these is the *Suite* of what were originally dance movements. Sonata-form itself developed from the more elementary shape of these dance pieces, and the Suite's design of alternating fast and slow movements was carried on in the later sonata. You can still hear the classical Suite form both at orchestral and instrumental concerts: examples by Bach, Handel, Purcell, and others are still in the repertoire. In the earliest days of instrumental art, suites were formed of all sorts of dance-movements, but gradually, by about the year 1700, as a result of experiment, certain rhythms had become accepted as most fit for inclusion. The Suite (sometimes called a *Partita*) contained about five pieces. It began with a *Prelude*, after which came an *Allemande* (a dance of German origin in moderate 4/4 time, beginning with a short up-beat); then a *Courante* (literally 'running': it was in 3/2 time, but sometimes the bars were divided up into two groups of three notes instead of three groups of two: there was also another kind of Courante in 3/4 without rhythmic complications), then a *Sarabande* (a dignified dance of Spanish or Moorish origin, 3/2), and a *Gigue* or *Jig* (a lively dance in 12/8).

Each of these dances, which were the basic movements of the Suite, fell into two sections, each of which was repeated. In the Gigue it was quite common for the second half to begin with the opening theme turned upside down. There were other dances of the Suite, however, which were also often to be heard: the *Gavotte*, a French dance in moderate *alla breve* time (that is, in 4/4 but with only two real pulses in a bar) which always starts on the third beat, and is commonly followed by a *Musette*, a piece on a drone bass imitating a *cornemuse* or bagpipe, after which the Gavotte is repeated; the *Bourrée*, also French, and rather like the Gavotte, but a little faster and beginning on the fourth beat (instead of the Gavotte's third); and the *Minuet*, in slow 3/4 time, which, as we saw in the symphony, was followed by a Trio or second Minuet. Less frequently included were the *Passepied* (originally Breton, in moderate 3/4 time), the *Rigaudon* (from the south of France, in quick 2/4, and consisting of three or four sections, each repeated), the *Siciliano* (a pastoral dance in 6/8) and the *Hornpipe*, the only English dance to appear. All these were movements of the old Suite: nowadays a Suite may consist of any number of movements, either in dance forms of any kind – and many new dances have appeared since the eighteenth century – or illustrating some poetic or pictorial idea. An even older dance, the *Pavane*, although it was not part of the Suite, was very popular in the sixteenth and seventeenth centuries and has recently been taken up again by French composers like Fauré and Ravel. The Pavane was a formal and stately dance, and may have taken its name from the Latin *pavo* (peacock) owing to the way the dancers' robes swept out like a peacock's tail; but since the name was originally Paduana or Padovana, it is more probable that it was merely a dance from Padua in Italy. The Pavane was usually followed by a gay dance called a *Galliard*.

Slightly later kinds of Suite, and nearer forerunners of the Symphony, were the Divertimento, Cassation, and Serenade, three very similar types of work. They each consisted of several movements, like a Suite, but except for a couple of minuets they did not include dance pieces: their first movements were in sonata-form, and they ended with a rondo. Haydn and Mozart wrote many such works, mostly very light in style and easily enjoyable at first hearing: indeed, as you might guess from the name Divertimento, their main purpose was to divert or entertain people in their leisure moments, often at outdoor parties.

OVERTURES AND SYMPHONIC POEMS

In the great majority of orchestral concerts the first item is an overture, which those of you who know some French may guess means something like 'an opening piece'. But in its time the word overture has meant many different things. During the seventeenth century it implied a composition in which a slow dignified introduction led to a lively movement, at the end of which a few bars of the slow introduction returned to serve as coda. Frequently a minuet followed. This is the pattern of some of the Handel overtures still to be heard. The final minuet dropped off first, and the classical opera overture of Mozart's day usually consisted of a slow introduction and a faster main movement. It was only very gradually that the idea spread that the overture should bear any relation in character to the opera which followed, although Mozart and, particularly, Gluck, realized the advantage of setting the mood of the work from the very outset. As late as the first half of the nineteenth century, however, Rossini was using the overture as just a conventional orchestral prelude which had nothing to do with the opera itself – so much so that he quite often actually made the overture to one opera do duty again for a totally different work.

With Beethoven and Weber, however, the custom came in of including in the overture actual themes from the opera, and Weber's overtures to *Oberon* and *Der Freischütz* and Wagner's to *The Mastersingers* not only wonderfully set the scene for the work to come but give us a foretaste of the music. (It is unfortunate that some inferior composers seized the opportunity of making the overture nothing more than

a hotch-potch of tunes from the opera. This was particularly
the case with writers of light operas or operettas.) Overtures
taken from their theatrical context were played so much in
the concert room that a new demand was created, and
from the time of Mendelssohn and Brahms to our own day
very many overtures have been composed specially for
concerts without a thought of the opera house. Mendelssohn's *Fingal's Cave*, Berlioz's *Roman Carnival*, Elgar's
Cockaigne and Walton's *Portsmouth Point* are examples. These
concert overtures may be in sonata form, or they may be
quite free, and many of them are based on some picture or
literary idea – in other words, they are illustrative or programme music.

Another type of programme music which is free in form is
the Symphonic Poem or Tone Poem. This was more or less
introduced by Liszt, but before him Berlioz had paved the
way by writing what seemed a contradiction in terms, a
programme symphony (the *Fantastic*), for the symphony has
always been thought of as essentially 'abstract' music. The
Fantastic Symphony claimed to represent the emotions and
disordered fancies of a young poet in the grip of a powerful
drug, who throughout his dreams sees his beloved's face.
In the music this becomes a theme which crops up in each
movement in a different guise, now calm, now distorted,
now mocking. This practice of 'transforming' a theme was
taken up enthusiastically by Liszt, who wrote many
symphonic poems (works in one movement) in which
themes would recur several times in various forms, first
perhaps appearing lyrically and finally returning in a blaze
of splendour. Transformation of themes, however, is not an
essential part of the symphonic poem, and mostly the story
determines the form of the music. For example, Smetana's
Vltava illustrates the course of a tiny streamlet through
the Czech countryside until it becomes a majestic river,

Strauss's *Till Eulenspiegel* the adventures of the gay rogue until he is caught, sentenced, and hanged.

SOLO INSTRUMENTS WITH ORCHESTRA

You all know the word *Concerto* – the films and the radio have seen to that – but you may be uncertain of its exact meaning. It's a work for a solo instrument or instruments with orchestra, but it isn't just *any* kind of work for that combination (and this is where the films in particular have given a completely false impression). It is a work in (usually) three movements, following a fairly clearly-defined form, and demanding from the soloist a certain amount of virtuosity (technical brilliance).

The concerto as we know it developed from a seventeenth-century form known as the *concerto grosso*, the Grand Concerto. You can still hear examples by Corelli and Handel, and Bach's popular *Brandenburg Concertos* are mostly of the *concerto grosso* type. In this kind of work (which was in three or four movements), a small group of players, often two violins and a cello, was contrasted with the full body of the orchestra, not for show as soloists but purely to obtain a pleasing change of tone-colour. The fact that some works exist by modern composers for string orchestra with a small solo group – Elgar's *Introduction and Allegro* and Vaughan Williams's *Fantasia on a Theme by Tallis* are examples – does not make them *concerti grossi*. By the time of Haydn and Mozart this small solo group had given way to one soloist, and as instrumental virtuosity increased, the solo part became more and more difficult, until now a concerto soloist's job is an extremely exacting one. (In the hands of unscrupulous showmen, who play to the gallery and who rank themselves more important than the music, the concerto may easily become an excuse for tasteless display.)

The three movements of the modern concerto are (1) an adaptation of sonata form, (2) a slow movement, and (3) a finale, often a rondo. Of these, the most characteristic is the first, which could be described as roughly like the ordinary sonata form except that, as the soloist and the orchestra share the thematic interest, it is common for the orchestra to present both subjects before the soloist enters, when *he* also gives out both subjects, often with decorations. This is known as Double-Exposition. There is one other very important and characteristic touch. Near the end, the orchestra halts and leaves the soloist to play a brilliant cadenza or free rhapsody on the themes of the work, after which the orchestra rounds the movement off. These cadenzas were for a long time intended to be improvised (for improvisation was an art formerly practised by all performers), but so many abuses crept in, and cadenzas became so much an opportunity for vulgar show unrelated to the work, that composers began writing their own cadenzas, and for at least a hundred years now this has been the rule. The long double-exposition also became too cumbersome, and Mendelssohn set the fashion for a much more compressed first movement, in which the soloist enters at, or very near, the beginning instead of patiently waiting for the orchestra to set out all the material first.

Before we leave the concerto, a word about two of its relations we sometimes meet in the concert hall, the *Concertstück* and the *Sinfonia concertante*. The *Concertstück* (concert piece) is what its title implies, a piece for solo and orchestra in one movement; it differs from the *Concertino* (little concerto) in that the latter is a complete concerto on a small scale. A *Sinfonia concertante* may be indistinguishable from a concerto (as in Mozart), or it may be a symphony with a solo instrument which is not, however, given opportunities for a display of virtuosity (as in Walton or Rubbra).

DANCES AND OTHER SMALLER PIECES

In instrumental music there is also to be found a large
number of shorter pieces in forms we have not yet mentioned. Some of these are in dance forms more recent than
those of the classical Suite; the *Waltz*, for example, needs no
explanation except to say that, as in the case of other dances,
the waltzes to be found in concert programmes, such as
Chopin's, were not intended to be danced to, so that their
rhythm may be less rigid than those for the ballroom. The
waltz developed from an earlier dance, the *Ländler*, of which
you may meet examples by Mozart or Schubert. Marches
also have their place in concert music, both gay ones (as in
Tchaikovsky's Sixth Symphony) and funeral marches (as in
Beethoven's Third Symphony, the *Eroica*).

Rather like a waltz in tempo, and by being in 3/4, but
different in character, is the *Mazurka*, a dance from Poland
in which the accent falls not on the first beat as in the waltz,
but on the second or third. Chopin wrote many mazurkas
for the piano, though some are more refined than the
original lusty dance. Another Polish dance is the *Polonaise*
or *Polacca*, a dignified 3/4 measure with a basic rhythm

♪ ♫ ♪ ♪ ♪ ♪ . Each country has its own dance rhythms,

but not many others have made their way into the repertoire
of serious music. Possible exceptions are the *Tarantella*, a
very lively dance in 6/8 from Southern Italy (which was
widely used as a form of exercise to cure people suffering
from the disease of Tarantism, believed to be caused by
infection from the bite of the Tarantula spider) and the
Bolero, a slowish but gay 3/4 dance from Spain with a very

pronounced and insistent rhythm ♪♪♪♪ ♪♪♪♪ ♫ –

there is a well-known orchestral example by Ravel. One or

two others are the *Polka* (from Bohemia), the *Czardas* (from Hungary) and the *Gopak* (from Russia).

There are a lot of free forms of various kinds, mostly in instrumental music. Don't jump to the conclusion that, because they are not clearly defined, they must lack shape. No good work, as we said at the start of this chapter, can exist without healthy bones, but the shape of the skeleton may vary as the composer's fancy dictates. Such forms are the *Caprice* and the *Fantasia* (Italian for Fancy – pronounced fan-ta-zē'ä), the *Impromptu* or *Improvization* (obviously written so as to sound spontaneous) and the *Intermezzo*, which, though strictly, according to its name, should be an interlude between two parts of a large work (an opera, say), may be just 'a piece'; it was a favourite title of Brahms's for piano pieces. A *Toccata* is a brilliant piece for a keyboard instrument, designed to show off virtuosity, and the *Étude* or Concert Study is much the same but based on some particular type of technical difficulty; in the hands of Chopin and Scriabin it touched great heights of poetry. A *Bagatelle* is a miniature, a *Ballade* a more extended work in poetic mood, and a *Nocturne* a slow, quiet piece suggestive of the tranquillity and beauty of night. A *Rhapsody* is entirely free in shape, but is based 'on' something – on a theme by someone (for instance, Rachmaninov's *Rhapsody on a theme of Paganini*) or on national and folk airs (like Dvořák's *Slavonic* or Liszt's *Hungarian Rhapsodies* – though, to be accurate, they were not Hungarian, but Gipsy, which is very different).

CANON AND FUGUE

There are two other terms you may come across in programmes which are really musical styles rather than designs. The first of these, the *Canon*, has nothing to do with either the Church or the battlefield, and is already known to you

all in a different connexion. You must have sung *Rounds* at
school, and enjoyed, as we all have, the way that the tune is
taken up at some point and combined with itself. This is the
special feature of the Canon too, although here it isn't
necessary for the new entry to come only at the end of a line,
nor need the new entry start at the same pitch. The writing
of canons needs, as you might imagine, a lot of careful
thought in order that the melody may be successfully combined with itself, and although there are some pieces
entirely in canon and called such, it is most usual to find
canon used purely as a device within a work. There is a
lovely canon between the violin and the piano in the last
movement of Franck's Violin Sonata, and there is an
interesting vocal canon in three parts by the Elizabethan
composer Byrd, which is called a 'perpetual canon' because,
like a Round, there's no reason why it should ever stop.

BYRD: NON NOBIS, DOMINE

You will have noticed something about this kind of writing which is entirely different from the great bulk of the music we hear. Instead of one tune with harmonies below it, which has been the most common style in music for the last two hundred years, the music of the period before about 1750 grew out of a style of singing in which everyone's part was of equal importance, and various strands of sound were woven together to produce the complete whole. This 'horizontal' writing for several voices is called Counterpoint, and it is unfamiliarity with this style which makes some people find listening to early music strange and sometimes difficult. But we shall have more to say about counterpoint later on. For the moment I want to mention a contrapuntal device which has retained its importance from early times right up to the present day, despite the radical changes in music that have taken place.

This device is called Fugue, and although many works are entitled fugues, it is not really a form at all. It would be more correct to talk about a piece *in fugue*. The Italian word *fuga* means literally 'flight', and in fugue the voices seem to be running after one another. At the beginning of a fugue, the voices or parts enter one by one with a subject, on which the whole work is based. The entries are alternately in the tonic key and the dominant (the key of the fourth below — for example, the dominant of C is G). During these entries (known as the Exposition of the fugue), the other voices may pass on from one to the other a phrase which combines with the subject, and which is therefore called the counter-subject. After the exposition, the subject reappears frequently in various keys. Towards the end the voices may all re-enter with the subject, overlapping each other — this is called *stretto*. An effect very commonly employed at the end is for the bass to remain on one note (either the tonic or the dominant) and for the other voices to build up a climax on this *pedal*, as it is called. The composer's name most associated with the Fugue is Bach, but there has scarcely been a composer of any standing at all who has not written in fugal style, and you may remember we said earlier that a set of variations often winds up with a final fugue.

IT'S WORTH KNOWING HOW MUSIC IS BUILT

Now I know that this chapter hasn't been easy reading, because we've had to cover a lot of technical ground. Don't worry about trying to remember it all at once; but it *is* important to understand how musical works are constructed, because it enables you to follow so much more easily what the composer is doing. Before the beginning of a work, try to find out its chief themes (the programme may give them, or else you must ask your teacher or look at the score for yourself), and you will find this a great help. But we will talk about other ways of getting the best out of your listening in a later chapter. For the moment just concentrate on recognizing the backbone of the composition: the smaller bones, though fascinating, are not so essential, and they will become more apparent as you get to know the work.

5
'Sweet Singing in the Choir'

'THERE is not any musicke of instruments whatsoever', wrote the great Elizabethan composer William Byrd, 'comparable to that which is made of the voyces of Men, when the voices are good, and the same well sorted and ordered.' And he went on, 'Since singing is so good a thing, I wish all men would learne to sing'.

Now it may be true that England does not produce large numbers of internationally famous singers (although we *have* had some fine voices), but this country has always been noted for the excellence of its choirs. In the twelfth century, part-singing was popular in Wales and what was known as Northumbria: to-day the same two areas, Wales and Northern England, are still famous for their choral singing. In all parts of the country, however, from at least the sixteenth century, communal singing has flourished, and it is worth noting that at all periods English composers have written their best works for voices; the Elizabethans wrote madrigals and motets, Handel (who became a naturalized Englishman) in his numerous oratorios always assigned a major role to the chorus, and recent composers like Elgar, Vaughan Williams, and Walton have written outstanding choral works. They were encouraged to do so, of course, by the fact that so many choral groups existed, and the story of the enormous growth of choral bodies and festivals during the last century in particular is a fascinating one, which I'm afraid is too long to be told here. Sufficient to say that singing is in the Englishman's blood, and if you have any voice at all and can read music, I hope that you too will join a chorus. There is a tremendous amount of pleasure to be had from it and, especially if you have a good conductor, it is a grand way of widening your musical experience.

TYPES OF HUMAN VOICE

I scarcely need to tell you that human voices, both male and female, vary according to the size of the vocal chords in their owners' throats. There are three types of men's voices and three types of women's – high, medium, and low. In this country most people belong to the middle category. Women's voices are called, in descending order, soprano, mezzo-soprano, and contralto, and men's voices tenor, baritone, and bass. I show below roughly what the compass of each voice is. It is interesting to notice that tenor parts sound an octave below their written notes – which I'm sure isn't realized by a lot of people who are puzzled by transposing instruments in the orchestra!

SOPRANO   MEZZO-SOPRANO   CONTRALTO

TENOR   BARITONE   BASS
(SOUNDING AN OCTAVE LOWER)

By the way, it is curious that some countries tend to produce particular types of voices. English voices are mostly mezzo-sopranos and baritones. We produce extremely few tenors. The Welsh and the Italians produce tenors in abundance, and the Russians go in for deep basses. It would be interesting to know exactly what effect different climates have on people's vocal chords.

Now, although there are six types of voices, it has always been the custom to divide a mixed chorus into four main groups – soprano, alto, tenor, and bass (with sub-divisions where needed), or S.A.T.B. as they are called for short. This means that the unfortunate mezzo-sopranos and baritones, who form the bulk of our choirs, have to decide whether to push themselves up a bit or down a bit, and are only really happy when their parts sub-divide so that they can get into their most comfortable register. There is no reason, of course, why composers shouldn't divide up the choir differently, if they feel inclined; and the Elizabethans (who had in mind small groups of singers, not the large masses of modern choruses) very often *did* feel so inclined. Besides mixed choruses, there are many fine male choruses to be heard, and these are divided up into two tenor and two bass lines. Female choirs (which are less common by themselves) usually split into three parts, two sopranos and contralto.

REHEARSING A CHORUS

There is one vital difference between orchestras and choruses which conductors and concert promoters forget at their peril. Orchestras are professional bodies, while choruses, with very few exceptions, are amateur. Whether in large choruses of two hundred or so, or small groups of about thirty, the great majority of choral music-makers in this country are ordinary people, who sing together for the love of it. And what difference, you say, does this make? Simply this – that for an orchestral concert one can summon the players for a rehearsal of three hours, and then put on a concert at which the conductor can rely on the players' alertness to follow his directions immediately and precisely; while for a concert in which a chorus is concerned, a long series of preliminary rehearsals is necessary, at times when people can get away from their work, so that the singers can learn their parts (which orchestral players read at sight).

It is not in the least unusual for a chorus to spend nearly a season of weekly rehearsals in learning one or two works of a size equal to that of a symphony. Of course there *are* some professional choruses, nearly all of small size, but their rate of progress is nothing like that of an orchestra. The atmosphere at a choral rehearsal is very much more informal. Where a brief direction is sufficient to guide or change the orchestra's reading of a passage, with a chorus it is necessary to enter much more fully into the whys and wherefores of everything. Since singing is so personal a thing, depending as much on the mental approach of the singers as on their technical equipment, the conductor must get his chorus into the right frame of mind, so that if they are singing something gay, their tone should not be tired and dreary, if something lyrical they should not be harsh, and if they are singing a tragic work they should not sound aggressively hearty and vigorous.

The difficulties of choral singing lie both in the music and in the words. Not only must musical points be watched as with an orchestra – and here questions such as attack and quality of tone, intonation, and balance are more than ever important – but the words must be easily heard and understood, and they must be sung with conviction of their meaning. As with solo singing, sometimes the claims of words and music pull in different directions, and the choral conductor's job includes deciding whether the musical shape or the meaning of the words is more important.

When a chorus takes part in what is primarily an orchestral concert, the conductor at the performance is quite likely not to be the same person who has trained the group all through rehearsals. Well-known orchestral conductors are usually too busy to be able to afford the time personally to take weekly choral rehearsals for every concert which calls for singers. Yet a chorus needs a regular conductor who can watch and guide its progress, quite apart from the fact that not all the concerts the society gives will be with orchestra. So there is a permanent chorus-master for each choral group, who prepares all the works and who conducts any concerts the chorus gives on its own, but who, if the chorus is to join in an item at an outside orchestral concert, hands over control to the orchestral conductor – who usually takes the last rehearsal before the chorus meets the orchestra. That's why you will often see on programmes 'Chorus-master, So-and-So; Conductor, Someone Else'.

CHORAL WORKS WITH ORCHESTRA

When we were talking about the orchestra, we mentioned that some composers had used the sound of a chorus singing, not to words but to vowels, as an extra orchestral colour. Now let's find out what kinds of music exist for orchestra with the chorus singing normally. There are a few – a very few – examples of symphonies with a chorus part. You may think this is rather strange, since I said that the symphony is 'abstract' music – that is, music which has nothing to do with words or pictures. However, I covered my tracks by saying that composers were at liberty to modify the normal forms to please themselves, and some composers have done so, successfully introducing choral movements into the framework of the symphonic form. Vaughan Williams, for instance, has written a *Sea Symphony*

in which each movement is a setting of words by the
American poet Walt Whitman and at the same time follows
the normal symphonic pattern – a sonata-form first movement, a slow movement, a scherzo, and a finale. Mahler
made several daring experiments with the form of the
symphony, bringing in voices; his Eighth Symphony is
indeed a work in only two parts, one a setting of a Latin
hymn and the other a scene from Goethe's *Faust*, and critics
have argued for years as to whether this can be called a
symphony at all. The most famous choral symphony, however, is Beethoven's Ninth – in fact, when people talk of *the*
Choral Symphony, they mean this one – and here the
gigantic finale is Schiller's *Ode to Joy*, set in what is basically
variation form.

By far the greatest number of works for chorus and
orchestra are on religious subjects, but of course there are
non-religious works as well, although there is often some
uncertainty about what they should be called. Their form
depends entirely on the words, as there are no set forms like
those of a symphony or a concerto, and non-religious choral
and orchestral works are either classed as *Cantatas* (which
means literally just 'something sung') or are not classified at
all and are known merely by their titles. Works in this class
which you may come across are Coleridge-Taylor's *Hia-
watha*, Elgar's *King Olaf* and *The Banner of St George*, and
Ireland's *These Things Shall Be*.

ORATORIO: A RELIGIOUS DRAMATIC POEM

The most popular kind of religious work for chorus and
orchestra, particularly in this country, is the *Oratorio*, and a
large number of choral societies seem to perform nothing
else. Most societies are composed of amateurs, and some
enthusiastically run their own affairs without professional

advice, but, although we admire their spirit, it must be admitted that in the choice of music a professional has – or should have – greater knowledge, and it is a pity that the 'oratorio only' organizations do not sometimes ask for guidance. For not only are there plenty of other kinds of works to sing, often more suitable for smaller bodies than an oratorio, which is a large-scale work, but, as people like to stick to what they know, the majority of choruses perform only about four or five favourite works. Now it is true that Mendelssohn's *Elijah* and Haydn's *Creation* are good works, and Handel's *Messiah* and *Israel in Egypt* great, but it is obviously silly to have dozens of performances of these up and down the country when there are plenty of others equally fine to choose from.

And what, I can hear you asking, *is* an oratorio, after all this? It is a dramatic poem on a religious subject, set for solo voices, chorus, and orchestra. The characters in the story are represented by soloists, but the work is not acted and is given without scenery or special costumes. The words can either be taken from the Bible or can be specially written. As usually given in this country, an oratorio unfortunately is only too often a dull affair, with a row of soloists ranged in front of the stage next the conductor, standing up just to sing their own bits, and the chorus singing away in an enthusiastic but un-subtle *forte* most of the time; but although it isn't acted, an oratorio is dramatic – that's to say, it tells a story – and, when you come to consider some of the stories on which oratorios have been written, it is quite amazing that they could ever be made dull.

Handel wrote a great many oratorios. They vary considerably in style, but there are certain characteristics common to all his writing which may need a little explanation. For example, the chorus sometimes takes part in the action as a

crowd of priests, Philistines, Israelites or such, and sometimes represents a quite impersonal body commenting on
the situation; or, as in *Israel in Egypt*, it may actually re-
count the story. In most Handel oratorios the story of the
action is put into the mouths of the soloists, and for this
purpose they are often given not a real melody but a kind
of cross between speaking and singing, in which the words
are practically recited, in the rhythm of normal speech.
This is called *recitative*, and is accompanied only by an
occasional chord, usually from the harpsichord or other
keyboard instrument. Before a piece of recitative gave way
to the next chorus or solo, it was a convention to have a
formal cadence something like this:

as if to say, 'That was just to get the story on a bit; now we
can spread ourselves and have some music'. And a soloist
would either continue with a commentary on the mood of
the action at that moment, or would progress slowly with
the story, set more formally so as to make a ternary musical
movement. Most Handel arias are in this ternary form (first
part – middle section – first part repeated). When it came
to choruses, he used a variety of forms, but very often wrote
in fugal style. So, you see, there is no reason why formal
patterns cannot be used for dramatic as well as for abstract
purposes, and some of Handel's fugues are most exciting –
for example, 'He trusted in God' from *Messiah*.

Messiah, incidentally, is far and away the most popular oratorio in this country, and certainly the work of Handel best known to the general public. Any Christmas-time will find it being performed in towns and villages throughout the land, and there must be tens of thousands of choralists who probably do 'know every note', as they proudly claim. Yet if you listen to it, you will hear that it is a most unusual type of oratorio, in that there are no characters to be represented by the soloists, and there is no narrative. It is, instead, a most beautiful work of contemplation and commentary on the Christian creed.

There is one custom in the performance of *Messiah* which will certainly catch you unawares unless you are prepared for it. At a performance given before King George II, the King was so moved by the Hallelujah Chorus (at the end of part 2) – about which Handel himself had said, when writing it, 'I did think I did see all Heaven before me, and the great God Himself' – that he rose to his feet. Seeing the King standing, the rest of the audience rose too. Since that time it has always been the custom to stand during the Hallelujah Chorus, and although nowadays some concert societies are trying to discourage the practice, it is still very widely followed.

Oratorio, of course, does not begin and end with Handel, nor do all the later writers compose along Handelian lines. The most famous of modern oratorio composers is Elgar, whose masterpiece *The Dream of Gerontius* is becoming increasingly popular, and whose other works are now finding champions. In Elgar's work there is no division into recitative, aria, and chorus; in fact, recitative in the old sense has ceased to exist; and the construction is far more symphonic, themes appearing and being developed throughout the work, the whole having a much greater continuity.

SACRED CANTATAS AND PASSION MUSIC

What is the simplest kind of music for choir you can think of? I would suggest a hymn. You may be surprised to learn that hymns play a quite important part in certain kinds of larger-scale works. Germany in the eighteenth century possessed large numbers of fine hymn tunes which were familiar to all churchgoers – and that meant to practically everyone. So it was quite natural that, apart from their use for congregational singing, the hymns should be drawn on for other forms of religious music. Bach, for example, wrote a great number of organ preludes on hymn tunes, decorating and developing the material in all kinds of ways to produce instrumental interludes of great beauty. You are quite likely to hear examples at an organ recital to-day, or, in arrangements, at a piano recital. The name for a hymn tune was a Chorale (pronounced ko-ral'), and as the word is spelt in German without the final *e*, some people have become confused, and think of a Choral-Prelude as if it were something to do with a chorus, when it is obviously for an instrument.

We said before that a cantata meant simply 'something sung', but Bach wrote a large number of *sacred* cantatas which mostly follow a certain pattern, and which make use of the chorale as an important element. Unfortunately there aren't as many performances of Bach's cantatas as there deserve to be, but extracts from many of them have become very well-loved (for example the aria *Sheep may safely graze*, or Bach's treatments of the chorales *Sleepers wake* and *Jesu, joy of man's desiring*), and it is worth knowing a little about them. The cantata in Bach's time was the chief musical point of the long church service, and, like the sermon which came immediately after, was based on the Gospel for the day. There would be about half-a-dozen movements, in verse for treatment as a chorus or aria, or in prose for recitative. The work usually began with a chorus, continued with solos and concluded with a verse of a chorale in which all could join. Sometimes, in addition, the first number of the cantata would be an elaborate setting of the hymn tune for chorus. The accompaniment for the cantata was always for orchestra and not for organ, for in those days orchestras were common in churches. It is a pity this is no longer so.

Chorales make their appearance, too, in Passion Music, a large-scale setting of the story of Christ's crucifixion, for chorus, soloists, and orchestra, very like an oratorio in size and general lay-out. It uses recitative, and the story is told by a Narrator. In Bach's two Passions (according to St Matthew and to St John) he is a tenor. When he comes to the words of any of the characters, they are taken up by a soloist representing that character. Interspersed with the drama of the crowd and the principals in the action are reflective and devotional arias, and chorales for the chorus, beautifully harmonized, whose words are commentaries on the situation. Performances of Bach's Passions are given in many places at Easter. You may find them a bit long, but they contain some of his most sublime music, and are in places really exciting dramatically. It is only rarely that you will come across settings of the Passion by composers other than Bach, although a poor work by the Victorian writer Stainer, called *The Crucifixion*, is sometimes still given, and this also introduces hymn tunes to break up the action.

LATIN CHURCH MUSIC

You won't need to be told that composers in all ages have written music for the service of the Church. Indeed, up to the seventeenth century the Church was the greatest patron of all the arts, affording musicians and painters a 'market' for their work. We have already seen that Bach's cantatas formed part of the Lutheran Church service. Now let us look at some of the types of music written for the Catholic Church, which nowadays may be heard, separated from their original context, in the concert hall. The most important is the Mass, the central point of the Catholic religion. Up to about the seventeenth century it was nearly always set for unaccompanied choir, and it is interesting that the musicians' term for unaccompanied singing, *a cappella*, actually means 'in church style'; while, from the time of Bach onwards, it has been customary to write for chorus (often with soloists) and orchestra.

Some of these settings – by Mozart, Beethoven, Schubert, and others – are extremely long and elaborate, and were in fact intended for the concert hall and not for church use at all, but some contemporary composers such as Vaughan Williams and Rubbra have gone back to the simpler *a cappella* style setting. In whatever style it is set, concise or elaborate, with or without orchestra, the Mass consists of five main sections (which are sometimes sub-divided). The words determine the mood of each movement, and as these Latin words are extremely well known and have been set again and again, composers can, and do, treat them with the utmost imagination and resource.

You will find it a help to know at least the general drift of each section as you follow a performance in the concert hall, and a good programme note will give you the words, but here are the five main sections: (1) *Kyrie* ('Lord, have mercy'); (2) *Gloria* ('Glory be to God on high'); (3) *Credo* (the Creed); (4) *Sanctus* ('Holy, holy, holy') and *Benedictus* ('Blessed is he'); and (5) *Agnus Dei* ('Lamb of God').

Another type of Mass, rather less frequently heard, is the

1. The London Philharmonic Orchestra at the Royal Albert Hall

3. Sir John Barbirolli at rehearsal

FAMOUS BRITISH CONDUCTORS

2. Sir Thomas Beecham at rehearsal

4. Sir Adrian Boult at rehearsal

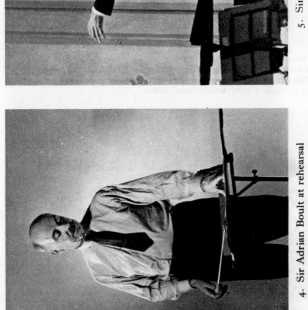

5. Sir Malcolm Sargent

FAMOUS BRITISH CONDUCTORS

6. A harpsichord of 1771. Like the organ, the harpsichord can give only the tone colour which is set in advance by its stops; and this cannot be affected by the performer's touch. The second keyboard is usually set to provide a contrasting tone colour.

7. The Griller String Quartet in a B.B.C. studio.

8. The violins, the most useful instruments in the orchestra.

9. The violas are larger and heavier than the violins.

10. The cello section. Notice the harps and the double-basses in the background.

11. The double-bass: you will see the player has to stand up to it.

12. The flutes. The second from the left is the piccolo.

13. Oboes and (extreme right) cor anglais. Notice the difference in length between the two instruments, and the longer curved mouth-piece of the cor anglais.

14. Clarinets: the mouthpiece is quite different from that of the oboe. The instrument nearest the camera is the bass clarinet.

15. Bassoons: the tube is so long that it is doubled back on itself. On the extreme right is a double-bassoon. Notice the horns sitting in the row behind.

16. The horn is 12 feet long and is coiled into a circle. You can see quite clearly the extra lengths of tube which are brought into play by the valves.

17. The trumpets: the valves are controlled by the player's right hand.

18. Close-up of a solo trombonist. His slide is extended to the second position.

19. The tuba's enormous bell is an impressive sight; but the instrument has a surprisingly mild voice.

20. Some of the extra percussion. Xylophone nearest the camera;
tambourine sitting on the glockenspiel; the side-drum (just visible);
the cymbals ready for action; the triangle hanging from the music
stand; and the bass-drum. There is a set of tubular bells behind the
centre players.

21. The harps. If you look hard you can just make out one of the
pedals which alter the notes' pitch.

22. The kettledrums or timpani: notice the tuning taps round the edges. Next to the timpanist stand the other percussion players: you can see (looking right to left) gong, bass-drum, cymbals, and side-drum.

Mass for the Dead, or Requiem. Most of the examples you are likely to hear are for chorus and orchestra; and the text is, of course, slightly different, leaving out the more joyful passages of the ordinary Mass and replacing them with other prayers. Here is a list of the usual movements: (1) *Requiem aeternam* ('Grant them eternal rest'); (2) *Kyrie*; (3) *Dies irae* ('Day of wrath'); (4) *Domine Jesu Christe* ('Lord Jesus'); (5) *Sanctus* and *Benedictus*; (6) *Agnus Dei*; (7) *Lux aeterna* ('Eternal light shine upon them'); and (8) *Libera me* ('Deliver me from eternal death'). There are many dramatic moments in the Requiem, and most of the settings to be heard nowadays were not designed for church use, though they may have been prompted by the death of some dear friend or relative of the composer. Mozart half completed one on his deathbed, and was haunted by the thought that he was writing a Requiem for himself. The examples by Berlioz and Verdi both seize on the dramatic possibilities of the text, and Berlioz in particular, using four brass bands in addition to an enormous orchestra and chorus, conjures up a terrifying picture of the Last Trump. There is also a very lovely work by Brahms, frequently performed, called *A German Requiem*. In spite of its title, it is not really a Requiem at all, but a setting of verses from the German Bible.

Before we leave this subject of musical settings of particular Latin hymns, there are four shorter works which should be mentioned. They can be heard in settings either for accompanied or unaccompanied choir – the *Ave Maria* (a hymn to the Virgin); the *Stabat Mater* (describing the grief of Mary at the Cross), usually sung in Passion week; the *Magnificat* ('My soul doth magnify the Lord'), a hymn from the Evening Service; and the *Te Deum*, a hymn of praise, often sung on some notable occasion such as a great victory or a coronation.

MUSIC FOR UNACCOMPANIED CHORUS

All this time we have been considering mostly works for chorus with an orchestra, but very many choral bodies give concerts on their own. It is true that some, having no association with orchestral players, try to get the best of both worlds by performing works to the accompaniment of the organ, but this is very far from satisfactory, and apart from being makeshift it is not a faithful representation of the composer's ideas – which, after all, is the first responsibility in any kind of performance. Far better to take the bull by the horns, and sing unaccompanied. The difficulty is that *a cappella* singing mercilessly shows up a choir's weaknesses of tone-quality and of intonation. But which is better, to conceal these weaknesses or to overcome them?

Some kinds of unaccompanied works have already been mentioned. Another form is the Motet, a contrapuntal composition on religious or serious words for chorus (without solos): you may hear examples by Bach or by English composers of Elizabethan times. But the great treasure for unaccompanied singing is the Madrigal. It flourished for only about thirty years in this country, about the turn of the sixteenth century, but in that short time hundreds of little masterpieces were turned out. A madrigal was short and very often dealt with topics of love. Some especially light-hearted madrigals had refrains of 'fa-la' and were known as Balletts (not to be mixed up with the later art of dancing), but some were serious, ironic, tragic, or even religious: in fact, the madrigal catered for almost every type of taste. All madrigals, both here and in Italy, where they were popular rather earlier, were essentially contrapuntal in style: that is, every voice was melodically of equal importance, and had its own very free rhythmic shape independently of the others. Imitations between the voices abounded, and the words were treated very expressively – almost pictorially, even. Words like 'weeping', 'dying', 'languish', 'merry', 'dancing', and so on, always received some characteristic treatment, and street-cries and the sound of bells were often imitated. The Elizabethan scene is vividly brought to our eyes in Morley's madrigal depicting the bustle at the arrival of the morris-dancers (*Ho, who comes here?*), or in the start of his *Fire! fire! my heart*. In fact, for sheer vitality and beauty the madrigal has a literature unsurpassed in any other field of music. People may tell you that madrigals are more fun to sing than to listen to, and to some extent that is true, but it is impossible not to feel their attraction. To our present-day ears their contrapuntal richness is a refreshing change from the bulk of the music we hear.

The modern equivalent short choral piece is known as a Part-song, and differs by being fundamentally homophonic – that is, the opposite of contrapuntal, with one part standing out and the rest harmonizing it. There are, of course, a large number of beautiful and attractive part-songs, but it would scarcely be an exaggeration to say that the more contrapuntal an unaccompanied choral piece is, the more interesting it is. Choirs also sing arrangements of folk-songs at their concerts, and fortunately there are quantities of excellent choral arrangements of tunes of all countries. There are a number of Scottish folk-songs arranged by Sir Hugh Robertson; Vaughan Williams and others have written a great many fine arrangements of English folk-songs; and Kodály has written delightful works based on tunes from his native Hungary. There is, in short, plenty to sing if you know where to look for it.

TRY SINGING FOR YOURSELF

Let me end this chapter by repeating the advice I offered you at the start. Do join a choir yourself as soon as your voice settles down. It's one of the easiest ways of making music (because you don't need the technical qualifications necessary to become an instrumentalist or a solo singer) and one of the most rewarding, for you get to know works that you wouldn't know otherwise, and get to know them more thoroughly than you would as a mere listener. Singing together is splendid training in the practice of music – and it's great fun!

6

Recitals

IN comparison with the amount of organization (and, in the case of orchestras, the expense) involved in a choral or orchestral concert, it is relatively easy to put on a concert by one artist. All that is necessary is to book the hall and arrange for publicity, tickets, and programmes, and the rest is up to the performer. No complicated arrangements for rehearsal are needed, no vast outlay, and, of course, there are far more solo artists than there are orchestras or choruses. So that it is not surprising that in, say, Saturday's *Daily Telegraph* (where it is the custom to advertise London concerts) there are more announcements of solo performers than of anything else. A concert given by one artist is called a recital, though we also count as 'one artist' a group such as a string quartet, or a violinist and pianist playing sonatas. Sometimes, also, two soloists will share a recital.

Recitals, in general, are of three varieties. They can be sponsored by a music society of some kind (such as the famous Manchester Tuesday Midday Concerts or the numerous music clubs up and down the country); they can be put on by an agent – most celebrities who are box-office attractions have dates arranged for them by managers or impresarios; or they can be arranged by the artists themselves.

PITY THE NEW ARTIST!

In the musical world of to-day there is always a large number of new artists who are trying to make their names, and the only way they have of bringing themselves to the attention of the public is to give recitals at their own expense and hope that an audience – and particularly critics, agents, and the BBC – will come and be impressed with their work. It is a heart-breaking job, for there are so many singers and instrumentalists of a high standard that competition is very keen, and the more concerts there are the less likely it is that the critics will be there. In London especially, there are far too many concerts. This week, actually as I write, there are twenty recitals and twelve orchestral concerts, which is by no means exceptional; and when three or four concerts take place on the same evening it is obviously impossible to go to everything one would like. So, in the case of new artists who are, so to speak, hanging out their name-plates, it is inevitable that the bulk of their listeners consist of friends and relations who come to 'make an audience'. The critics are as anxious as anyone to welcome new talent – there is nothing more cheering than to come across a musical 'find' among the crowds of candidates for fame – but they cannot be in several places at once, and anyway have very little space allowed them in the Press nowadays. They are most likely, therefore, to go to the important concerts, leaving the new artists to wonder sadly whether it is worth while giving recitals at all. If you are just starting to go to concerts you may prefer not to take a risk which may or may not turn out to be a good one. Instead you will go to one of the first two classes I mentioned. The music club is probably a good bet. The committee organizing it wants to maintain a standard, and is likely to get reputable artists; and you are not at the mercy of agents cashing-in on a celebrity's name.

CELEBRITY CONCERTS: THE COMPOSER IS THE REAL STAR

You will undoubtedly want to go to hear the celebrities, and quite right too, for they have probably earned their fame, and we all want to hear things done as well as possible. But the world of music is not like the film world, where the personality of a star is of prime importance, and where it is the custom to go to see the star almost regardless of the work in which he appears. This attitude is indeed adopted by some people when it comes to music, but the principle is foreign to any real art. After all, it is the music written by the composer which is really important, and the concern of the executant artist is to interpret it as faithfully as he can. The greater the artist, the more faithful the interpretation. But some celebrities (which is not at all the same thing as saying 'some great artists') are more interested in their own personalities, and, like certain star conductors, think in terms of 'their' Beethoven, 'their' Brahms, and so on. So let me give you this piece of advice: if you find a recital being advertised with the performer's name very large and without any mention of the programme, beware! for it means that the music is being subordinated to the star, and that is fatal.

IT'S HARD WORK BEING AN ARTIST

From books and films you may have got the impression that the musical celebrity's life is a glamorous one – one long round of publicity, travel, and applause. That view overlooks the realities – the endless tiring journeys, the irregular meals, the sense of homelessness that comes from moving from hotel to hotel, and above all the hard work and the necessity of practising, the nagging awareness that one must appear in good form, that critical ears will be listening to every note, that one cannot afford to be ill and disappoint one's public, and that (if a singer) one dare not even have a cold. Nearly all the great celebrities are unanimous in finding life in the constant limelight both worrying and wearisome. Do not think that these stars don't have to work hard all the time, that they are supermen who just walk on to a platform and, without turning a hair, rattle off from memory a whole programme of difficult pieces. As to working, that fine violinist Mischa Elman is reported as saying: 'If I don't practise for one day, I notice it; if I don't practise for two days, other violinists notice it; and if I don't practise for three days, everybody notices it.'

An artist's self-assurance and apparent lack of nerves are due to the long, hard concentration and application which are necessary to rise to the top in any art, but most great artists will confess that in fact they are always nervous before a recital; only confidence in the thoroughness of their preparations enables them to control their feelings. Being human, however, they have their off-days and make errors like anyone else, but they can never forget that they have their reputation at stake.

VIRTUOSITY AND A SILLY HABIT

The interpreter's duty, as we have said before, is to present to the audience the composer's music with as little distortion as possible. To do that, two things are necessary, technique and artistic insight, and neither is much good without the other. The truly great artist will have both equally; lesser performers will have them in varying degrees. It is obvious that all the musical understanding in the world is useless without the means of expressing it. As Rachmaninov (himself one of the very greatest artists) put it, 'Without technique there *is* no interpretation'. But the possessor of a brilliant technique often so dazzles the public that it forgets to look for the musical imagination behind it all.

Virtuosity, which should be a means to an end, becomes an end in itself; and we must always be on our guard not to be blinded by mere show – for the number of performers with more technique than understanding is very great. Not that listening to sheer virtuosity isn't exhilarating, but it's the same kind of exhilaration and fascination as that produced by watching a man riding a bicycle along a tightrope – we know that it's risky and that the performer is playing on our half-fearful wonder. But whereas the acrobat is completely fulfilling his job by showing his skill, the musician is letting the skill take pride of place over the musical thought, which is the real essential.

A word about the habit of giving bouquets at concerts. You will see it both at star recitals and, sometimes, at recitals by new artists. It's silly really, and as it's perfectly obvious that the flowers are sent in by friends or, in the case of young artists, by proud relatives, it deceives nobody into thinking any the more of a performance. It was, I think, Bernard Shaw who pointed out the impossibility of an audience offering spontaneous tributes, and who referred ironically to the custom of well-bred people of always taking a bouquet with them to a concert on the off-chance of wanting to present it!

PLANNING A RECITAL PROGRAMME

As in any other type of concert, there is a definite art in building a recital programme, so as to produce contrast while yet allowing a concert some character of its own. The artist, having to carry the whole programme on his shoulders, must not be allowed to become too exhausted, and so it is usual to make up the recital into about four groups and to have, besides a real interval, pauses of two or three minutes between the groups during which he can leave the stage and relax. A group will consist either of one work, such as a sonata, or a number of works by the same composer or in similar styles – for example, a singer might present a group of songs by present-day British composers. That much is easy: it is when it comes to providing variety and balance between the groups that the problems begin.

Let us think of some of the ways a programme might be built up. We could have a whole recital devoted to the works of one composer, designed to show the variety and scope of his music. It would be simple, for example, to devise a programme by Chopin, Beethoven, Bach, or Brahms, each of whom could provide a wide range of choice. A common plan for a mixed recital is to have the works in date order, so as to show how style and technique changed as the art of music developed. Or the programme could be planned to illustrate one particular period, with examples of music by different composers working at that time: these historical programmes are far more interesting to musicians than a miscellaneous collection of works put together just to show off the artist's talent.

A singer may offer songs by composers of different nationalities, singing each group in a different language, in order to show the effect that the character and rhythm of a language have on the music of that country. It is a remarkable thing that, despite the great differences of style that may exist between composers of the same nationality, it is nearly always possible to recognize a song by its musical character alone – that is, without any words – as being French, German, Italian, Russian, or English. An interesting idea, recently carried out in some song recitals, is to group together different settings of the same words, for many poems by Shakespeare and Goethe, for example, have been set over and over again.

In a way, although they don't possess works that last for twenty minutes or so, like a sonata, singers have the advantage in building programmes, for they can draw on a far greater variety of music than can any other type of soloist. But if they sometimes feel that greater continuity is desirable, one solution ready to their hand lies in the Song-Cycle. This is a series (of any size) of songs by the same composer written to form a single unit, a group on a central theme, in which literary or musical ideas may return throughout the work. Some famous song-cycles are: Schubert's *Fair Maid of the Mill* and *The Winter Journey* (two long works lasting about an hour each), Schumann's *Poet's Love* and *Woman's Life and Love*, Vaughan Williams's *On Wenlock Edge*, and Mussorgsky's *The Nursery*.

ABOUT APPLAUSE

It is natural to want to applaud if we have enjoyed a musical work, though it is sometimes difficult to know whether we are applauding the performer or the music (that is to say, the composer). If the audience has been greatly moved by a work, there may be a short silence after it is over, in which nobody will care to break the spell. This silence is rightly regarded as an even greater tribute; it shows that the performance has lifted the audience right out of itself. But we need to be discriminating in our applause: it should never be allowed to become a mere habit. Our reaction, in fact, should be in proportion to the pleasure we have received. I'm not saying that if the performance has not pleased us at all we should descend to booing or hissing, as they do in France and Italy, but we needn't clap at all, and a half-hearted response is one of the biggest rebuffs a performer can receive.

In England, such are our curious ideas of sportsmanship, we are often misled into being too kind. Many people applaud an artist for 'a brave try', as it were, and there have been innumerable instances of performers who have unblushingly tackled music obviously far beyond their powers, in some cases actually coming to grief during the performance, who have been rapturously received by the audience in a mistaken belief that in any circumstances it is praiseworthy to battle against fearful odds. A musician who is not up to performing a certain work, by reason of his lack either of technique or of understanding, is ruining the music by 'having a smack at it' in public, and should be not praised, but blamed, for an artistic crime.

In the case of a song, however thrilled we may be, we shall of course not start to applaud until the song is over, which is to say when both the singer and the accompanist have stopped. The piano part is in many cases quite as important as the vocal line, but in any event it is the height of ignorance and vulgarity to break in on the pianist's last few bars, if he has to continue after the voice part. Quite as vulgar is the horrible habit of some singers, especially in the cheaper kinds of music, of holding on a high note just before the end much too long and loud in the hope of forcing applause from those who don't know any better. This playing to the gallery, though fortunately less widespread than it used to be, is still shockingly prevalent, particularly in the provinces.

By the way, while we are on the subject of applause, I might just add that it isn't done to talk during the performance, even to say something appreciative to your neighbour; but if you feel you will burst if you don't say it, then *say* it quietly and don't whisper. A whisper carries much further and is far more irritating. You may have heard that an important recording once taken of a public concert was utterly ruined because during a momentary pause in the music the sensitive microphone picked up a woman in the hall whispering to her neighbour, 'Of course, we always fry ours in dripping!' And may I say one more thing – please don't tap your feet in time to the music: you've no idea how infuriating it can be to other people.

SHOULD THERE BE ENCORES?

During a song-cycle, one does not applaud the individual songs; nor does one clap after the movements of a sonata, suite, quartet, symphony, concerto, etc. At an orchestral concert, a movement of a big work may last some time and, if you do not know the work well, appear to be complete in itself, but, unless you want to find yourself the only person in the hall clapping, try to keep your enthusiasm until the end. Customs have changed, and this convention of not applauding single movements was not always in force. A century ago it was quite in order for the audience even to demand an encore of any movement that took its fancy – and very flattered the composers felt. Even in performances of oratorios and other sacred works, where normally nowadays the rule is no applause at all (out of respect for the subject), it was customary to clap any part that was liked: at the first performance of *Elijah* in 1846 in Birmingham, Mendelssohn wrote in delight that 'No fewer than four choruses and four arias were encored'.

Nowadays no one asks for, or expects, encores at an orchestral concert of any kind, a sonata recital, or a programme of string quartets. At recitals made up principally, or partly, of short works, such as a song recital or a miscellaneous programme of piano works, it is, however, still habitual to give encores, and some artists would be highly offended if they weren't asked for them. Serious-minded musicians have protested that the encore habit is a foolish one. Not only are encores sometimes given without sufficient justification, but frequently they bear little relation to the programme that has gone before, and are often mere unworthy attempts to drag forth applause by means of virtuoso effects. It would be far more dignified for the artist to say, in effect, 'Here is my complete programme: when I have played the last piece in it, that's the end'. The argument goes on: 'When an actor comes to the end of a play, he is not then expected to come before the curtain and give a couple of recitations'. This is all true enough, but so long as audiences continue to clamour for encores, and performers feel that they haven't 'gone down well' unless they have been recalled for more, so long shall we have this habit with us. An encore need not, however, be inartistic. Instead of some piece of empty display calculated to provoke a frenzied reaction, it is possible to give some quiet piece which will send the audience away satisfied and contented.

MUSIC FOR ROOMS OR FOR SMALL HALLS

There are certain types of music, as for example orchestral works, which need a large hall so that the mass of sound has room to breathe, as it were. To put them into too small a room would be like cramming schoolboys into infants' play-suits – even if they went in at all, they would be horribly cramped and acutely uncomfortable. On the other hand, a small group of players like a string quartet is far happier in smaller surroundings. In too large a hall the players feel all the time that they have to exaggerate and broaden everything they do in order to fill the space, with the result that their performance becomes out of proportion and loses the intimate quality which is part of the charm of this type of music. String quartets and similar groups are really most at home in a fairly large private room, and many enjoyable quartet performances do actually take place in the friendly atmosphere of people's homes. Hence this music is known as chamber music or, as it has been called, 'room music' – intimate music which is free from all public fuss and playing to the gallery, and which people can listen to in an easy mood of relaxation and friendliness.

Many people have no idea what is really meant by chamber music, but have got it firmly fixed in their heads that it is wildly dissonant modern stuff, so that, being frightened, they take up a ridiculous attitude and write in alarm to the papers about 'this awful chamber music' without finding out what they are talking about. The odd thing is that a recent radio programme called 'Music in Miniature', consisting of movements from chamber works, was extremely popular among the very people who made most fuss!

However, not all of us have the opportunity of hearing quartets in our homes, which is the ideal; professional players must play in public to earn a livelihood, so chamber concerts are held in small halls throughout the country – in big ones too sometimes, though these bigger halls are never really suitable.

The string quartet, to which we have referred so often, consists of two violins, viola, and cello, and has a very large repertoire, almost every composer of any standing having written for it. There have been string quartets made up slightly differently, with a bass instead of a cello, or with other variations, but in the great majority of cases the instruments are, as I have said, two violins, viola, and cello. There are, however, many other types of ensemble in chamber music besides string quartets: string trios (violin, viola, and cello), piano trios (piano, violin, and cello), piano quartets (meaning quartets including a piano, not groups of four pianos!), string quintets, clarinet quintets, and so on in very great variety. When does a group cease to be chamber music and become a small orchestra? There is no hard-and-fast dividing line, as it partly depends on the point at which a conductor appears to become necessary, but groups of more than nine are rare, and after that they might well be considered chamber orchestras.

VOICE AND PIANO AS EQUAL PARTNERS

Another type of music which also, because of its intimate character, is better in a small hall is that kind of song known as a *Lied* (which is just the German word for 'song' – pronounced *leed*). *Lieder* (the plural) are commonly considered the finest kind of songs, but it is rather difficult to define exactly what they are. The term is applied to songs by certain German composers – Schubert, Schumann, Brahms, Wolf, and Strauss are the chief – in which the voice and the piano are treated on equal terms and both are at the service of the poem. The aim is not merely to produce a beautiful and singable melody; it is, instead, to capture the mood of the words, and to this end the song is conceived as a whole, the voice and the piano combining to produce the effect. There is no question in lieder of having a vocal melody plus an accompaniment. Sometimes the piano has the tune, the characteristic rhythm or the main interest, and in a great number of cases its part is not only as difficult as, but more difficult than, the voice line. Any false impression you may have had about this will soon be put right once you hear Schubert's *Erl King* or Strauss's *Serenade*.

Songs in languages other than German, even when they are of a similar type, are not called lieder; but such is the wealth of variety and of musical interest among German lieder alone that complete recital programmes are frequently made up of them.

THE MAN AT THE PIANO

At everything but piano recitals, there is a second person involved who has it very largely in his power to turn the whole affair into a success or a failure. He receives little attention, certainly less than he deserves, even from some of the artists themselves. His name on the posters is printed in small type. If he is mentioned at all by the critics, he rarely receives more than a phrase at the end of the notice, to the effect that he was 'sympathetic'. Who is this? On the programme he is stated as being 'At the piano' – not even playing it, you notice. Yet the accompanist is, from the musical point of view, a very important person indeed, and first-rate accompanists rank with the finest soloists in the world.

Consider what they do. They have to be prepared to play song accompaniments of every kind and accompaniments to pieces for every type of instrument, as well as to take part in sonatas and chamber music. Much of this work is technically difficult, and from the point of view of interpretation always as difficult as the soloist's part. A good accompanist is not just a helper, 'following' the artist discreetly and unobtrusively. He is a partner on equal terms, who by training and previous rehearsal comes to the performance with the same ideas – or ideas on the same lines – as his soloist.

Not only must soloist and accompanist be entirely at one over such things as tempo, rhythmic stress, and phrasing, but in every detail the accompanist must merge his personality into that of the soloist and, with a kind of supersensitive telepathy, actually think with him and see with his eyes. Each artist will react on the other, so that they will make a *crescendo* or a *rallentando* together. A stolid singer may even be fired by his accompanist's urge, for the man 'at the piano' quite often needs to take the lead and gently prod his soloist into life, or, of course, restrain him if he shows signs of exaggeration.

Perhaps it hadn't occurred to you that the pianist pays as much attention to the meaning and mood of the words as the singer, for they guide his ideas too? If the singer should make a mistake, perhaps skipping part of the song, the accompanist has to cover things up smoothly so as to keep up the continuity and conceal the disaster as well as possible. The slightest hesitation, weakness, or lack of response would be fatal.

Some soloists will play with piano accompaniment works which were written for orchestra. In these cases the accompanist should know the scores and try to convey something of the orchestral effect in his playing. It is not sufficient for the pianist even to know the enormous repertoire of songs in one key only. Different artists may sing the same song in different keys, which may mean extra technical problems for the pianist. He must be ready to transpose a song at sight (that is, to play it immediately in a key different from that in which it is written) if the singer should suddenly decide that the song would be more comfortable a semitone or so up or down. Unless the request is obviously unreasonable, the accompanist takes this kind of thing for granted. Even without these added complications, consider what it must be like to play a song for dozens of different artists, each with slightly different ideas of tempo and interpretation. In every case the accompanist must remember the details and must appear at the performance completely at ease with his soloist. Now imagine the same thing for a whole programme of songs, and you will have some idea of the number of things the pianist has to carry in his head!

The accompanist's attitude has to be a strange one: he has both to immerse himself in what he is playing and, with another part of himself, to remain outside it – immerse himself so that he can give full rein to his playing and provide a stimulating partnership, and remain apart so that he can analyse the effect and judge what modifications, if any, are necessary actually during a performance. With all these responsibilities, he is also expected to put heart into his soloist if the latter is nervous. He may be feeling just as nervous himself – possibly more so – but were he to show it too there would be no feeling of confidence before the pair stepped on to the platform; and so accompanists as a class steel themselves never to show their qualms.

You may see now why I said that the accompanist has it in his power to ensure the success or failure of the concert, for an inadequate player can let down the best possible soloist in a hundred different ways, whereas a good accompanist, though he cannot make a success of a bad artist, will at least minimize his faults, mask his worst mistakes, and guide him unobtrusively so that he appears better than he really is.

FROM MEMORY OR FROM MUSIC?

You sometimes come across the fashion of playing accompaniments from memory. Our best accompanists, when asked their opinions about this, are loud and unanimous in their disapproval. 'How *can* anyone,' they say, 'play for every conceivable kind of soloist night after night and keep every detail of interpretation as well as of the printed copy in his head? Besides, what happens in an emergency, if the soloist does something wrong and one has to cover up for him?' So that seems to be *that*.

Orchestral conductors nowadays frequently conduct from memory, and as they are more or less running the show, there is no great harm in this *if* – and only if – they have perfect memories which retain every intricacy of the score. (There is one famous conductor of the present day who always stands before the orchestra with his eyes shut!) But again there remains the question, how can they immediately take charge and put matters right if anything should go wrong in performance?

In the case of soloists, the same difficulty does not apply. On their own, they have to get out of any trouble by themselves and conceal any breakdown by their musicianship and quick thinking. Conventions are odd things, however. Although concertos are played from memory, it is an accepted thing to use the copy for any chamber music. Most soloists prefer to work without a copy because they feel freer that way. The presence of the printed page before their eyes seems to hinder them from becoming completely absorbed in the music. Still, in special cases where it is essential to be absolutely exact, as for example in recording, where, once done, the performance has to remain for all time, most people prefer to play from music. There is nothing really in it either way. Some people seem to imagine that it looks bad for an artist to have a copy at a concert, but if he is going to feel happier with it, it would be stupid to make things insecure for himself just for the sake of appearances. After all, remember that this fashion of playing from memory is only about seventy years old. A notice in *The Musical Times* in 1873, referring to a celebrated pianist, said his recitals 'created an excitement which must be partly credited to the fact of his performing entirely from memory', while six years later it was stated that 'such mental efforts are, indeed, not now altogether uncommon among executive artists, but they never fail to act as a surprise'.

7

The Men Who Wrote the Music: Part One

WHEN you go to a concert of any kind, you should always know in advance what you're going to hear. You wouldn't go to a theatre, for example, without finding out if you were going to see *Hamlet* or the Crazy Gang. You would want to get yourself into the right frame of mind for listening. This mental preparation is particularly important for music, because its whole style and nature have changed so considerably in the course of the last three hundred years, which is, for all practical purposes, as far back as people go for most musical programmes to-day. I cannot, even very briefly, run through the how and why of the development of music during this period – that would take more space than this whole book – but if you are interested to see how music developed (and it's a fascinating story), I have suggested some more books to read on page 175. In the next three chapters I tell you a little about some of the more important composers whose works you may hear, and suggest which works of theirs you might try first.

We have already spent some time in finding out what is implied by the various forms and titles of musical works, but composers at different periods have used different forms or have treated old forms in new ways, so that if you know something of a composer's background, nationality, and the general character of his music, you will have a good basis on which to start listening. Experienced concert-goers have only to see the composer's name on the programme to know roughly what the music will be like in style (though of course it doesn't follow that every work by a great composer will be a masterpiece). They will know not only whether it will be ancient or modern, but, in addition, something of the character of the composer and hence of his music, which is an expression of his personality.

THE COMPOSER'S PLACE IN SOCIETY

The problem which every composer has had to face is how to make a living by his writing. He has always needed a 'market', someone for whom to compose, who needed and would accept the products of his brain. Up to about the seventeenth century, the greatest patron of composers, as of artists of all kinds, was the Church, and the enormous bulk of music of that time was therefore written for the service of the Church – Masses, motets, etc. The advent of Protestantism meant a change in the type of music required, but the Church still remained a powerful patron of music. In the eighteenth century, the aristocracy of the various and numerous Courts in Europe were all vying with one another as patrons of the arts, and a composer of this time often lived in the service of a prince or a nobleman as a kind of superior Court servant, writing music for his employer's amusement, both for private use and for semi-public events like weddings and fêtes.

With the spread of revolutionary and democratic ideas which followed the French Revolution, aristocratic patronage became less and less important as the aristocracy itself thinned out. New markets began to be available in the public opera houses and in the big music publishers, who were enabled to set up in business by the great growth of public concerts and the consequent increase in the numbers of those interested in music. The rise of popular virtuosi, the manufacture of cheap instruments, the practice of publishing works at prices all could afford, the growth of musical education, the spread of choral societies, the emergence of the ballet as a popular entertainment, all contributed to provide a wider audience for the composer. In our own century the passing of the Copyright Acts, which stipulates that for any public performance a certain sum has to be paid by the concert-giver to the composer for the 'right to perform' (in this country these fees are collected and distributed by the important Performing Right Society), and the appearance of the gramophone, films, and radio, have made the composer's lot far more secure and given him greater opportunities than ever before. But even now it is still impossible to live by composition alone unless one is famous and very much played. Nearly all composers have to eke out their income by teaching or by performing in public. In Soviet Russia and in some other modern Sovietized countries, the State itself has become the greatest musical patron, owning its own publishing-house, running concerts and operas, and subsidizing composers.

The above sketch is necessarily a very brief outline, but it shows how composers have worked during the centuries for different purposes and in different conditions, and, as we shall see, they have had to cut their coats according to their cloth; or, shall we say, the various people who have paid the piper have called different tunes!

MUSIC BEFORE 1700

In the normal way, we hear at concerts very little music composed before 1700, not only because nearly all of it was written for the Church, but because the style seems to most people both difficult to follow and apparently shapeless. However, after being neglected for centuries, many early works are just beginning to be appreciated. The patient

efforts and researches of musical scholars have enabled us
to see unaccustomed beauties in them.

We will begin, appropriately enough, in our own country.
In the year the Spanish Armada was defeated (1588), an
important collection of madrigals was published by the
great composer BYRD, and from then on for about thirty
years, through the last years of Elizabeth's reign and into
the reign of James I, the madrigal flourished as a favourite
form. Among the numerous madrigal composers the most
attractive is, perhaps, MORLEY, who specialized in cheerful
subjects and who popularized the ballett or 'fa-la' type.
This period also saw the beginnings of instrumental music
(for until then music had been conceived only for voices),
and there are several collections of keyboard pieces – little
dances, variations on popular tunes, fantasias, etc. – written
by Elizabethan composers, including, besides Byrd and
Morley, FARNABY, WILBYE, and others. The keyboard
instruments of the time were the virginals and the harpsichord. The latter was a slightly later and more elaborate
version of the virginals: they differed from the piano in
having the strings plucked by quills instead of struck by
hammers. It was at about this same time, too, that the violin
family began seriously to displace the earlier viols, though
the first composer for the violin whose works we hear nowadays is CORELLI, who wrote sonatas (which are in fact
short suites). His smooth, gentle style of playing went out of
fashion at the start of the eighteenth century. The Frenchman COUPERIN (who was organist in Louis XIV's private
chapel at Versailles) was another pioneer of the Suite, and
very many of his little harpsichord pieces have fanciful or
descriptive titles, like *Sister Monica* or *The Little Windmills*.

Apart from music for the Church and instrumental music,
the seventeenth century also saw the birth and growth of
opera. Louis XIV had, as his Court composer of operas and

ballets, the Italian-born LULLY, some of whose dance-tunes are occasionally heard, while in England during the Restoration the most famous figure was Henry PURCELL, who was at the Courts of Charles II, James II, and William and Mary. Besides writing a great deal of music for the theatre, he was also organist of Westminster Abbey, and wrote numerous works for royal occasions. His instrumental suites and sonatas are not much heard these days, but many of the dance-movements from his stage works, and several songs (often constructed on ground-basses) are frequently performed.

For an introduction to Purcell's attractive rhythmical style, try the dances from his 'Fairy Queen' (an adaptation of the 'Midsummer Night's Dream' in which not a word of Shakespeare is set!); and for songs on ground-basses either 'When I am laid in earth' from the opera 'Dido and Aeneas', or the lovely 'Evening Hymn'.

THE WONDERFUL YEAR 1685

The first date that most people remember in music is 1685, which is taken as a convenient starting point for the music which is generally performed to-day. In this year three important composers were born – Bach, Handel, and Domenico Scarlatti, the first two in Germany and the last in Naples.

The works of SCARLATTI are the earliest harpsichord works to be heard at all frequently to-day. Although he was a Neapolitan, he spent most of his life in the service of the King and Queen of Spain, and his 600-odd sonatas, which he wrote to play himself, not only show a wonderful liveliness and freshness of invention but a remarkable standard of keyboard technique. His harpsichord sonatas are all short works in one movement, unlike the later sonata-form we mentioned in Chapter 4, but it is possible that they may originally have been played in pairs.

People often think of Bach and Handel as two inseparables (like Gilbert and Sullivan!). The truth is that they had very little in common beyond greatness and the same country and year of birth. BACH lived his life in Germany as a hard-working provincial organist, writing vast quantities of cantatas and organ music for use in church; he was deeply and sincerely devoted to the service of religion. He spent a short time as Court musician to a princeling and to a duke, during which time he had opportunities for writing secular instrumental music and orchestral works. He finished his days as Cantor of a school in Leipzig, training choirboys, instructing in music, and generally supervising the music-making of the churches of the town.

Bach's music was considered old-fashioned even by his sons (many of whom were also composers) because it was contrapuntal and complex in style at a time when tastes were changing to the more direct, simple harmonic style made popular by the Italian opera composers. He was keenly interested in technical problems, which in his hands never became dry or dull, and he left not only dozens of separate fugues but some famous collections – the so-called *Art of Fugue*, where the same subject is used for fourteen different examples in various styles, and the *Well-Tempered Clavier*, two separate sets of twenty-four preludes and fugues in all the major and minor keys. He popularized, by means of the '48', a then fairly new system of tuning keyboard instruments. Up to that time, they had been so set as to be playable only in certain keys, but in this new system (called Equal Temperament), all the twelve semitones of the scale were made slightly out of tune by the same amount, so that no key would be more out of tune than another. Although there was at first some opposition to this spreading-over of out-of-tuneness, Equal Temperament has stayed with us ever since. Bach's greatest works are his two *Passions* and the superb *Mass in B minor*, one of the great masterpieces of all music.

If you want to make a start on Bach, try one of the Brandenburg Concertos or the Third Orchestral Suite in D (which contains the well-known Air). If you get a chance to hear the B minor Mass or the St Matthew Passion, you shouldn't miss it, even if you only stay for a part of it. You should try to hear some of the Chorale Preludes and of the '48'. And you would enjoy keyboard works such as the Fifth French Suite in G.

In contrast to the local reputation of Bach, who was known only inside Germany and whose music was then completely neglected for over a hundred years, HANDEL was a cosmopolitan figure who travelled widely and who was one of the best-known personalities of his time. As a young man he played the violin and harpsichord at the Hamburg opera house, and then travelled in Italy as a performer and composer, making a great reputation. These tours had a strong influence on his style, and brought him into contact with all the leading musical figures, including Corelli. He then became *Kapellmeister* (Court musician) to the Elector of Hanover, but he still hankered to travel, and sought leave to visit England. Here again he made a success as an opera composer but, overstaying his leave by two years, found that by a trick of fate his patron had become King of England as George I. The King's displeasure at Handel's desertion soon vanished, however, and Handel became a favourite in Society. He later became a naturalized Englishman. For nearly twenty-five years he directed, with varying success, companies for the production of Italian operas, writing over thirty works. At times he was extremely prosperous, at others almost bankrupt. Eventually the public got tired of Handel's rather stiff type of opera, which dealt only with legendary kings and heroes, and they demanded something more lively and less heroic. His business rivals were making difficulties, and Handel, realizing that taste was changing, decided to give up opera and transfer his energies to writing oratorio instead. He had some success with *Messiah* in Dublin and *Judas Maccabaeus* in London, and gradually recovered prosperity with a whole series of oratorios. He was buried in Westminster Abbey. Handel's operas have long since disappeared from the repertoire, though we often hear songs from them such as *Where'er you walk* and *O ruddier than the cherry*. Some of his orchestral *concerti grossi* and violin sonatas are played to-day, but his fame now chiefly rests on his oratorios, above all *Messiah* and *Israel in Egypt*, and so we are apt to think of him, not as the operatic composer he was, but, like Bach, as a writer of religious music. Handel's style is much simpler and more harmonic than Bach's, though he could write fugues with the best, and in his arias he used the *da capo* form almost exclusively.

You will certainly get a chance of hearing 'Messiah', wherever you live. As Handel is fairly easy to understand, it doesn't greatly matter what you start on. Try to hear one of the violin sonatas; look out for examples of his operatic songs; and get to know the 'Water Music' for orchestra (which is always being played).

MUSIC IN VIENNA

The next composers to claim our attention made Vienna the centre of their activities, but before we get to them we must spare a glance for the Englishman Thomas ARNE, who wrote operas and theatre music for Drury Lane and Covent Garden. His instrumental pieces are mostly forgotten, but some of his songs are still sung, and his *Rule Britannia* (from a patriotic stage work) will always be with us.

At much the same time in Vienna, GLUCK was setting

out seriously to reform opera by adopting a freer technique, giving a greater rôle to the chorus and aiming at greater continuity of action than had been possible with the string of formal arias favoured by Handel. The only pieces by Gluck you're likely to hear these days, however, are one or two extracts from his most famous opera *Orpheus*.

With HAYDN we feel at last that our feet are on firmer ground, for his quartets and symphonies are known and loved to-day. After studying in Vienna and working there for a time, he spent thirty years of his life in the service of the Esterházy princes, writing music for the fine orchestra they maintained, and establishing his fame throughout Europe. On the death of his patrons, he visited England twice to give concerts, and then returned to Vienna, where he lived long enough to hear, in his last year, the guns of Napoleon's besieging armies. His was a genial and kindly character, which is reflected in his music. Haydn's importance lies in his adoption and development of sonata-form, and in his formulating the pattern of first-movement – slow-movement – minuet-and-trio – rondo for the symphony and the string quartet. His music is elegant and beautifully proportioned, but never shallow, and always full of vitality and humour. For all his aristocratic style, his healthy peasant origins peep out in his sturdy minuets and in the cheerful dance-like rhythms of his finales. He wrote over a hundred symphonies and quantities of chamber works, though we hear only about a fifth of them. His oratorio *The Creation* is still very popular, and pianists enjoy his melodious and gay sonatas.

Many of Haydn's works have acquired nicknames: you can start with any of the following symphonies: the 'Surprise', the 'Farewell', the 'London', the 'Oxford', or the 'Clock'; and, among his quartets, with the 'Lark', the 'Sunrise', or the 'Emperor' (so called because it includes variations on the lovely national hymn of Austria, which Haydn wrote).

Haydn had a great influence on another Austrian musician twenty-four years his junior – MOZART. This extraordinary genius produced music in almost every form, and showed an amazing mastery in every style. He first made his appearance as a child prodigy, touring all the Courts of Europe as harpsichordist and composer (he was writing little pieces at five, symphonies at eight, and operas at ten!) and creating a tremendous sensation in Austria, Germany, France, England and, later, Italy. There is no doubt that his musical brain was altogether exceptional, and he seems to have had the faculty of composing completely in his head so that he could then sit down and write, say, an orchestral score, straight out in one sitting without any hesitation.

After numerous tours, he returned to his native town of Salzburg, where he smarted under the harsh treatment of his patron the Archbishop, and finally succeeded in leaving him (being in fact unceremoniously kicked out). He then settled in Vienna and tried to make his living. Although his symphonies, concertos, and operas pleased everybody, including the Emperor and the nobility – his opera *The Marriage of Figaro* was the rage of the town and was played and whistled everywhere – he could obtain no appointment, and was driven to teaching and writing dance-music to try to keep himself going. (There were no fortunes to be made in those days from publishers or in performing rights.) Despite all his hard work, it was impossible to make ends meet. He died ten days before his 36th birthday and was given a pauper's burial.

It is scarcely possible even to indicate all that Mozart did for music. He developed the art of orchestration, bringing the still new clarinets into the orchestra and writing for them with loving imagination, as well as using trombones with overwhelming effect in his operas *Don Giovanni* and *The Magic Flute*: his orchestral writing is a miracle of grace and clarity. He brought the symphony to a new pitch of perfection, discarding Haydn's formal slow introduction to the first movement and generally showing a far greater range of emotion. He was the first great master of the concerto, writing several works for the piano (which was now superseding the harpsichord) and for the violin, besides concertos for the horn, clarinet, bassoon, and flute. He developed the technique of opera, securing far greater characterization and dramatic intensity than his predecessors, and showing an original genius in the organization of his scenes: he can also be said to have created German opera with *The Abduction from the Seraglio* and *The Magic Flute*, for until then 'opera' had meant Italian opera. And we have still not mentioned his chamber music, his church music, the Requiem or his instrumental works! The apparent ease and calm of Mozart's music is very deceptive: some people have been deluded into thinking it merely charming and elegant, but in fact his simplicity conceals a wonderfully skilled technique, and below the formal beauty of his writing there is often deep and passionate feeling.

It is difficult to know where to start with Mozart, so much is beautiful, but you should hear the symphonies in E flat and in G minor, some of the concertos and the chamber music (try the Clarinet Quintet first and then the G minor Piano Quartet), and as much of the operas as you can, even if it's only the overtures. After that you can please yourself. The 'K. number' after the name of a work by Mozart instead of an opus number is merely the number in Koechel's complete catalogue of his works, and is used as an aid in identifying it.

THE FIRST OF THE INDIVIDUALISTS

The music of BEETHOVEN, though at first something like Mozart's in style (and he was a pupil, for a short time, of Haydn), very soon showed itself to be utterly unlike what had gone before. To understand the reason for this, we must think of the times in which he lived. They were times when exciting new ideas were about, ideas of liberty and the brotherhood and equality of Man, ideas which brought about the French Revolution and which had a profound effect in every other country of Europe. To artists, and in particular to those with noble ideals like Beethoven, such theories only increased their ardour. Beethoven felt the courtly, formal musical style of Mozart and Haydn to be unsuitable for the expression of his aspirations: on all sides he was reaching out towards freedom. In fact, he intended to dedicate his Third Symphony to Napoleon, the personification of the revolutionary spirit, but he was so disgusted when his hero, abandoning ideals of equality, made himself Emperor that he tore up the dedication, which now reads only 'To the memory of a great man'. His one opera (*Fidelio*), too, deals with the defiance and overthrow of tyranny.

Beethoven's revolutionary sentiments, though well-known, did not prevent him from being befriended and patronized by various Viennese noblemen. This was also the time of the rise of the great publishers, and Beethoven was fortunate enough to have them at hand as well as his noble patrons. The most staggering thing about Beethoven is that at about the age of thirty he became totally deaf, a terrible affliction for any musician, and doubly so for a sensitive and fiery nature like his, and yet it was only *after* this that he composed nearly all his greatest music. His deafness and his sense of frustration and isolation drove him to live only for his composition and to be completely careless of his surroundings and his person. The notion of composers as wild and unaccountable characters can undoubtedly be traced back partly to his example.

His passionate individuality is clearly visible in his music,

and the daring originality of many of his works alarmed and
baffled his contemporaries. He seemed to scorn conventions,
beginning his First Symphony with a discord, bringing in a
horn phrase in the Third Symphony in an obviously wrong
key, and writing a Ninth Symphony of enormous proportions and difficulty in which the finale, after experimenting
with various ideas, turns into a choral setting of Schiller's
Ode to Joy (once again, proclaiming the brotherhood of
Man). He transformed the concerto from its Mozartian
style into an expressive form in which (as in the E flat or
the G major Piano Concertos) the soloist could set the mood
of the work at the very beginning instead of waiting for a
long orchestral exposition. He gave a new freedom to
sonata-form, whether in sonatas, symphonies, or quartets,
by greatly extending the development section and by experiments with the number and style of movements. He discarded the Minuet and Trio, setting in their place the
Scherzo and Trio in which he could express his own boister-
ous sense of humour. He put the art of orchestration on an
absolutely firm basis, and in his Fifth Symphony introduced
the trombones as normal members of the symphony
orchestra. In his slow movements, particularly in the late
quartets, he reached heights of sublime thought and poetry
which have rarely been equalled. He was indeed a composer who can truly be termed great.

*The choice open to anyone coming new to Beethoven is embarrassingly
wide. You can't go wrong with any of the symphonies (though I recommend the Eighth, the Seventh, and the Fifth to start with) or the earlier
piano or violin sonatas. You will have plenty of opportunities of hearing
his overtures 'Egmont', 'Coriolan', and what is called 'Leonora No. 3'
(the third overture written for his opera), which are good examples of his
dramatic style, and you should not miss the lovely Violin Concerto.*

A GREAT SONG-WRITER

We are still concerned with music in Vienna, but our next composer, SCHUBERT, who had a deep reverence for his great contemporary Beethoven, was quite unlike him in character. He was an amiable, modest, cheerful person who was content to live with his friends, making music for and with them, and not troubling too much about profound intellectual matters. Unlike Beethoven, who kept note-books in which he jotted down musical ideas as they occurred to him and laboriously worked over and polished them, Schubert seemed to pour out ideas in an inexhaustible flow. He would dash off a song at a sitting, oblivious of his surroundings and of conversation around him: *Hark, hark, the lark*, for example, was written on the back of the menu-card at a tavern where he sat with friends. His gift of melody was prodigious, and in his songs he caught to perfection the mood of the poems, setting them to music in which, besides the voice, the piano played an important part. He wrote the wonderful songs *Margaret at the spinning-wheel* and *The Erl King* – two of the greatest masterpieces of the entire song repertoire – at the ages of 17 and 18 respectively. Schubert never held an appointment of any kind, and publishers were uninterested in him until his friends had some of his songs engraved at their expense. Before he died, at the tragically early age of 31, he had written over 600 songs and a great deal of chamber, orchestral, and instrumental music; perhaps more, as a critic has sadly said, than the world will ever have time to know.

The Schubert works you are most likely to hear are his piano pieces, which are not, however, a very good introduction: far better is his in-cidental music to 'Rosamunde', or the famous two-movement Eighth Symphony (the 'Unfinished'). Some of the songs you probably already know, and among the chamber music you might start with the 'Trout'

Quintet (so called because one of its movements is based on his song of that name) or the Octet, which is full of light-hearted gaiety.

TWO OPERATIC COMPOSERS

Meanwhile, interesting things were happening in the world of opera. A conductor named WEBER had ambitions for a national German opera, and in his own works set a new line for others to follow. The turmoil of ideas following the Revolution had turned the thoughts of poets and novelists away from classical stories of ancient heroes towards characters and ideas of their own time, and towards what was called Romanticism – an interest in nature, the picturesque, the supernatural, and the emotional. Weber introduced this new spirit into the theatre with his operas *Der Freischütz* (*The Marksman*), *Oberon*, and *Euryanthe*. The first of these was a sensational success everywhere – in London it actually ran at three theatres at the same time – and it created an extraordinary atmosphere of supernatural horror with its story of evil demons and with its vivid music. You can still hear the overture and one or two arias. Another popular Weber overture, *Oberon*, similarly conjures up a wonderful sense of the fairy world.

At the same time a vivacious and witty Italian, ROSSINI, was conquering Europe with his operas. Having aroused enthusiasm in Venice, Rome, and Milan, with *Tancredi* and the comedy *The Barber of Seville*, he turned to Vienna, then the most musical city in Europe, where again he had a triumph. Schubert and Beethoven admired his sparkling music, and he for his part tried to get up a subscription to aid Beethoven; but Weber, intent on setting German opera on its feet, had no time for this new Italian craze. From Vienna Rossini went to London, where he became the idol of Society (and where he sang duets with

George IV), and then to Paris, where, gauging his audience's tastes exactly, he turned to more serious works on the theme of liberty, such as *Moses in Egypt* and *William Tell*. In concert halls to-day Rossini's overtures are still very popular. You will hear in most of them a favourite trick of his, a long and gradual orchestral *crescendo* which whips up excitement: in fact, so fond was he of this effect that he was nicknamed 'Signor Crescendo'. He was, despite his quick and alert mind, a very lazy man, and a curious thing about him is that, after *William Tell*, he practically gave up composition although he lived for nearly another forty years.

8

The Men Who Wrote the Music: Part Two

THE nineteenth century was now well under way, Romanticism was in full swing, and change was in the air. Artistic thought in Europe was under the spell of Shakespeare, Byron, and Walter Scott. No composer was more fully in tune with the spirit of his age than the temperamental Frenchman BERLIOZ, a brilliant musical journalist with extraordinary imagination and adventurousness. Berlioz has always been a bone of contention among musicians. Whatever the opposition at first to a new composer (and most serious composers have started by upsetting their hearers by their new ideas), musicians eventually come to some agreement about the standing and value of his work, but disagreement has raged about Berlioz from his own time to the present day, one faction regarding him as an original genius and the other as a crude amateur with grandiose ideas. Grandiose his ideas certainly were. He had an astonishing sense of orchestral effect and a flair for new orchestral colours, and he startled the musical world with works written for enormous forces, like the *Requiem*, which demanded, in addition to a gigantic orchestra, four brass bands, or the *Funeral Symphony* which called for 120 wind instruments over and above those in the basic 130-strong orchestra. It is not often anyone can afford to mount these monsters nowadays, but much of the rest of Berlioz's orchestral music is performed – his masterpiece, the theatrical *Fantastic* Symphony, the viola concerto entitled *Harold in Italy*, and the overtures *Roman Carnival*, *Beatrice and Benedict*, *The*

Corsair, and *Benvenuto Cellini*. But his two great operas on *The Trojans*, the dramatic cantata *The Damnation of Faust* and the lovely oratorio *The Childhood of Christ* – his best works – are mostly neglected.

COMPOSERS FROM THE NEW MIDDLE CLASS

Not all musicians were revolutionaries. As at any other period of history, different characters reacted to the same events in different ways, and much depended on their environment and on their circumstances. Composers are always individuals, though it is easy to forget that a name we see on a programme represents a person who really lived, with likes and dislikes, ideas and a personality of his own.

With the growth of industrialization and the new wealth derived from commerce, a prosperous middle class was coming into existence, and it was from this well-to-do background that there came the German composer MENDELSSOHN. He was handsome, kindly, popular, well-read, and talented, and the fact that he never had to struggle to earn a livelihood, as so many other composers had to do, is reflected in the fluent, melodious, tasteful, sentimental, and rather shallow music that he wrote. He exerted a very considerable influence on music as a conductor and composer in Leipzig, where he founded the Conservatoire, in Berlin, where he wrote a good deal of theatre music, and in England, where he was enormously popular and where his 'gentlemanly' person and music made him Queen Victoria's favourite composer. It was largely due to his efforts that Bach's works were rescued from complete oblivion, and he was always ready to help his fellow-musicians. As a composer he excelled at light and dainty scherzos such as those in his incidental music to *A Midsummer Night's Dream* and in his *Octet*, but he was also capable of more robust humour and of imaginative mood-painting, as in the *Midsummer Night's Dream* Overture (written when he was only 17), the *Italian* Symphony, and the *Hebrides* Overture (*Fingal's Cave*). His oratorio *Elijah* is still widely performed, and the immense popularity of his Violin Concerto shows no sign of diminishing.

Another figure from a slightly lower level of this same middle class, who was born the year after Mendelssohn, was SCHUMANN, a composer at his best when writing for the piano, used either solo, with the voice, or in chamber music. He was fortunate in that his wife was a fine pianist who did much to make his work known. He was a tireless crusader for the new music, and edited a famous paper in which he wrote under several pen-names, attacking what he called the 'Philistines', the stick-in-the-muds. He was among the first to hail the music of Chopin and Brahms. His own works, from having been very popular, have now somewhat declined in appeal and are thought rather sentimental and whimsical, but this does less than justice to his poetic fancy, his ability to portray a mood in a few bars of piano music, and the beauty of his songs, which rank not far below Schubert's in the *lieder* repertoire.

You may already know some of Schumann's music for young people, the 'Scenes of Childhood', the 'Album-leaves', or the 'Album for the Young'. Now try to hear some of his more important piano music – the 'Fantasy Pieces' and particularly the suite 'Carnaval' (in which the Philistines and Schumann's characters from the paper he edited make their appearance in sound). The Piano Quartet is a vigorous and poetic work you will enjoy, and the Piano Concerto is extremely popular.

THE PIANO COMES INTO ITS OWN

By this time the piano was becoming an extremely popular instrument. Composers were beginning to exploit its peculiar qualities, and a school of virtuosi aiming at brilliant finger-work was coming into existence. Schumann was fascinated by the effects obtainable with the sustaining pedal. At almost exactly the same time a pianist of French-Polish extraction was introducing a new conception of piano-playing, aiming at poetical effects of 'half-lights' and at exquisite embroidery. This was CHOPIN, the best-known of all writers for the piano, and one who scarcely wrote anything for any other instrument. He was touring as a soloist when news came of the unsuccessful Polish revolt against Russia and the consequent occupation of Warsaw, his home. So he fled, like many other Poles, to Paris, which was now one of the great musical centres of Europe. Here he played his own music and gave lessons to rich and titled ladies (sometimes of the new nobility who had come into being as a result of banking and commerce). He introduced dance-rhythms of his native Poland into his music in the *Mazurkas* and *Polonaises*, and experimented with new harmonic and rhythmic effects. His music, refined and delicate, is mostly in shorter forms, with such titles as *Ballades, Impromptus, Nocturnes*, etc. His health was poor, and for some time he was cared for in Majorca by the strange woman writer George Sand; but the damp climate made him worse, and on a visit to Scotland and London in 1849 he was obviously in his last illness.

An equally bold experimenter in writing for the piano, and a virtuoso of the very front rank, fiery where Chopin was dreamy, was LISZT, a Hungarian who led a loose and extravagant life in his youth and later became an abbé (which didn't make much difference to his way of living!). His playing caused a sensation throughout Europe, and he himself exercised a strange fascination upon his audiences. He was lionized and fêted everywhere. This constant flattery had the worst possible effect upon him as a composer, for it turned his thoughts away from their natural nobility towards flashy display. From the technical point of view, not even Chopin worked such a revolution in piano writing as Liszt. He exploited every possible effect of the instrument, and for sheer brilliance his music has never been surpassed. His *Hungarian Rhapsodies* and other piano pieces are always being included in recital programmes, and the two Piano Concertos are also frequently to be heard, but we hear less of his orchestral works and songs, which are free from the temptations of display, than we should. He introduced the form known as the symphonic poem (his two best-known are *Les Préludes* and *Mazeppa*), and most of his orchestral works are 'programme music'. He made use of the device of 'transformation of themes' (see page 77) to obtain greater continuity.

OPERA IN GERMANY AND ITALY

Liszt's 'transformation of themes' ran parallel to a technique used in opera by his contemporary Richard Wagner, whom he befriended and helped (as he helped many other musicians – Liszt was the most generous of men). Wagner, a firebrand revolutionary who was constantly in trouble for his political opinions and often in exile, a most unlovable and unscrupulous character and a monster of selfishness and ingratitude, nursed gigantic schemes for German opera, or 'music-drama', as he called it, counting all the elements of opera – music, poetry, scenery, stagecraft – as of equal importance. To this end, he wrote his own *libretti* on German heroic folk-legends, setting them to music which was continuous throughout the work instead of being split up into separate arias, choruses, etc. To make his long involved sagas easier to follow, and as a means of stressing dramatic continuity, he adopted a principle of 'leading motives' attached to characters and ideas which recurred on each appearance or mention of that character or idea. Wagner's innovations did not stop there. He pushed chromatic harmony to what then seemed its furthest limits, and his grandiose schemes included a group of four long and immensely difficult operas, entitled *The Nibelung's Ring*, to be played on four successive evenings, needing an orchestra of a size unheard-of in opera, for which some of the instruments in the brass family had to be specially constructed.

Audiences found his music not only interminable but noisy and discordant, and for years it was the subject of the most violent discussion. By an astounding stroke of luck, however, Wagner attracted the attention of the half-crazy boy king Ludwig II of Bavaria, who supported him and enabled him to proceed with his most ambitious project, the building of a special theatre in which to perform his operas. This Festival Theatre at Bayreuth became the centre of a Wagner cult in which his music, once reviled, was listened to with almost excessive reverence by his worshipping admirers.

Operatic music does not really come within the scope of this book except in so far as it is performed at concerts. The only non-operatic piece by Wagner to be heard (and it is a good introduction to the composer's style) is the charming 'Siegfried Idyll'. Despite Wagner's aim to make his operas continuous, various extracts are in fact detached and performed in the concert room. The best orchestral extracts with which to start are probably the Overture and 'Dance of the Apprentices' from 'The Mastersingers of Nuremberg', the exciting 'Ride of the Valkyries' from 'The Valkyries', 'Forest Murmurs' from 'Siegfried', and the Overture to the earlier opera 'The Flying Dutchman'.

It so happened that Italy's greatest operatic composer was active in Italy at the same time as Wagner in Germany – the humbly-born VERDI, who wrote nearly thirty operas (of which about a dozen are in the repertoire) and whose masterpieces *Otello* and *Falstaff* were composed at the ages of 74 and 80 respectively! During Verdi's youth, Italy was under the oppressive rule of Austria, and he first made a name for himself by writing works with plots dealing with patriotism and freedom. These were warmly received by the public, but constantly landed him in trouble with the authorities, who insisted on his changing the characters and places in his operas *Rigoletto* and *A Masked Ball*. (After the peace which followed the short Austro-Italian war, Verdi became a senator in Cavour's government for five years.) At first his music had shown merely vigour and a great gift for broad flowing melodies, but later, taking romantic instead of heroic subjects, his style was to be marked by a greater richness of harmony and orchestration and a more sensitive feeling for character. He wrote *Aïda* for production in Cairo to celebrate the opening of the Suez Canal, and – although he admired Wagner's music – was displeased when it was called Wagnerian by some critics. For not only did he feel that Wagner expressed the awakening nationalism of Germany, but, with the example of the Franco-Prussian war before his eyes, he had the vision to realize that this new Germanism spelt war for Europe. In present-day concert halls, various arias from his operas are popular, but little else of his is heard, with the one exception of his thrilling and dramatic *Requiem*.

VIENNA AND PARIS AGAIN

Back in Vienna the whole city had gone waltz-mad, and was idolizing a father and son, both named Johann STRAUSS, who were the most famous writers of dance-music of the time. The younger Strauss, a most prolific composer, known as the 'Waltz King', is still pre-eminent to-day from such pieces as *The Blue Danube*, *Accelerations*, and *Tales from the*

Vienna Woods, as well as for his operettas *Die Fledermaus* (*The Bat*) and *The Gipsy Baron*, the overtures of which are very popular.

There was no more enthusiastic Strauss-fan than a serious-minded, rather surly composer who was a friend of the Schumanns – BRAHMS. (In fact, his delightful vocal *Love-song Waltzes* were inspired by Strauss.) He was in style the complete Romantic – individual, emotional, and melancholy and genial by turns – but he clung to the classical traditions of harmony and form (he wrote symphonies instead of the new Lisztian symphonic poems), and he was made the figurehead of the anti-Wagnerian movement (somewhat against his will), which may have brought him prominence more quickly than he would otherwise have achieved it. His output was considerable, and he wrote particularly well for his own instrument, the piano – works which demanded technique, but were far more solid than Liszt's. His *lieder* and his chamber music are in the top of their class, and his symphonies and orchestral works, if they show no outstanding feeling for orchestral colour, are firmly constructed, contain some fine music, and are most satisfying to listen to. His Violin Concerto is one of the world's masterpieces.

> There is a lot of Brahms to choose from, but some of it is rather mature to understand at first. I suggest starting with some of the shorter piano pieces, called *Intermezzi*, *Rhapsodies*, or *Ballades*. For orchestral music you should try the '*Variations on a theme of Haydn*' and the '*Academic Festival*' *Overture* (based on student songs) before tackling the symphonies. For the chamber music perhaps the best approach is through the Horn Trio and the Clarinet Quintet.

If Vienna was crazy about Strauss, the rage of Paris was the operetta composer OFFENBACH, who turned out over a hundred gay, light stage-pieces. Another tuneful writer, though in rather more serious vein, was BIZET, one or two of whose orchestral works are to be heard these days, such as the *Children's Games* Suite and the light-hearted little Symphony, besides extracts from his operatic masterpieces *Carmen* and from his incidental music to *L'Arlésienne* (*The Maid of Arles*). Bizet died before his colourful Spanish opera *Carmen* became successful. His contemporary SAINT-SAËNS, who lived to be 86, was hailed with enthusiasm in England and the United States as well as in his own country. He composed too quickly and wrote too much, but his workmanship was admirable, and the easy, if sometimes empty, brilliance of his writing proved very attractive to audiences of the time. You are quite likely to meet his orchestral tone-poems *Danse Macabre* and *Omphale's Spinning-wheel* and his humorous descriptive fantasy *The Carnival of Animals*.

A very different type of composer living in Paris was the Belgian FRANCK. He was a modest, simple, lovable, and devout man who spent the greater part of his life as an organist and professor of the organ. His best works were written late in life, and he had to wait a long time for any recognition. His music, which owes much in feeling to organ style, is extremely chromatic in its harmony, and his melodies are curiously unenterprising. Although no one could have been further removed than he from the extravagant fashionable world of Liszt, his harmonic flavour is not dissimilar, and he not only wrote symphonic poems after the Liszt pattern but, as in the Symphony and the much-loved Violin Sonata, adopted the device of 'cyclic' form (see page 73). One of his works that you should certainly hear is the attractive *Symphonic Variations* for piano and orchestra.

NATIONALIST COMPOSERS

All this time there were only two main styles of music, German and Italian. French composers had not yet really evolved a distinctive national style of their own, and English composers still less. But with the spread throughout Europe of patriotic ideas, people in other countries began to turn to their own national legends and national history, and composers sought an idiom in which to express these ideas. There was, in every country, something to draw on in the folksongs and traditional songs of the people, and fresh blood was brought into the body of music by the use of this kind of material in the more out-of-the-way countries.

We have already seen how Chopin used rhythms of his native Poland, but he was not the only one to draw on national sources, nor, as it happened, was this nationalist spirit to take its lead from Poland, but from Russia. About the same time as Chopin produced his first compositions, GLINKA in Russia was writing a patriotic opera *A Life for the Czar*, and, wishing to differentiate between Polish and Russian groups of characters in the work, drew on Russian popular music. Some of his aristocratic audience sneered at his 'coachmen's music', as they called it, but they were in a minority. There is nearly always 'local colour' to be found in Glinka's works, and if you hear his lively overture to *Russlan and Ludmilla* you will realize at once that it has a flavour different from any German or Italian works you've ever heard. Glinka, however, is more important as an influence than as a composer. A group of his disciples known as the 'Mighty Handful' took up his ideas enthusiastically and brought them to the notice of the rest of Europe, which was beginning to tire of the Romantic style and was ready to welcome something more pungent.

The most important members of the group were Balakirev,

Mussorgsky, Borodin, and Rimsky-Korsakov. BALAKIREV'S brilliant piano piece *Islamey*, one of the most difficult works in existence, is full of the barbaric glitter of Asiatic Russia. MUSSORGSKY was the most original of them all, but always something of an amateur. His *Night on the Bare Mountain* is a wonderful piece of imaginative orchestral scene-painting, and you may also hear his descriptive piano suite *Pictures from an Exhibition*. BORODIN was another composer under strong Eastern influence – his Symphony in B minor is full of vivid effect, and there is a picturesque tone-poem called *In the Steppes of Central Asia*. Extracts from his opera *Prince Igor* are often heard, and the charming *Nocturne* from his Second String Quartet is deservedly popular.

RIMSKY-KORSAKOV, the most self-assured and pro-fessional of the group, was a master-hand at orchestral scoring, and his *Scheherazade* is quite electrifying in its effect. He also wrote a most brilliant and exciting *Spanish Caprice*, following the example of Glinka, who had written a work on Spanish national themes. Spaniards might not accept this national colour, any more than they accepted Bizet's *Carmen*, as genuinely Spanish, but it formed the basis of the popular notion of Spanish style.

Rather outside the Mighty Handful and their ideas, though not unsympathetic to them, was another Russian more Westernized in his outlook – TCHAIKOVSKY. He was a melancholy and introspective person, and his music tends to be nervy, like the man himself, although he possessed a rich vein of poetry, and he could appear colourful and gay if he wished. A wealthy widow with whom he corresponded, but whom he never met, supported him and enabled him to devote himself entirely to composition. Towards the end of his life he took to touring as a conductor of his own works, at which he proved very successful in England and the United States. He had an unfailing gift for melodies of an emotional kind, and his music is so rich in rhythmical life and subtlety that it is not surprising that he was a successful composer for the ballet, an art which from his time onwards was going to need the help of serious musicians instead of the theatre hacks who had provided the music up till then.

> There is a Tchaikovsky craze at the moment, with the result that certain works, like the First Piano Concerto and the Sixth ('Pathetic') Symphony, are grossly over-played. Nevertheless they are very typical of him, as are the popular suites from his ballets 'Swan Lake', 'Nutcracker' and 'Sleeping Beauty'. A couple of attractive orchestral works to start on are the Fantasy Overture 'Romeo and Juliet' and the Serenade for Strings. Of his songs the well-known 'None but the Weary Heart' is characteristic.

NATIONALISM IN OTHER COUNTRIES

Other countries were not slow to follow the Russians' example. In Bohemia (which we nowadays call Czechoslovakia) SMETANA, though he had been brought up on German methods and had worked in Sweden for some time as a conductor and pianist, was imbued with strong patriotic ideas, and not only helped to found a National Opera House but produced for it a whole series of Czech works, both patriotic dramas and comedies of peasant life. Of these operas, the only one at all well known outside his own country is the gay and tuneful *Bartered Bride*, of which the Overture is frequently played. Orchestral programmes often include also some of his cycle of six tone-poems called collectively *My Country*, the best known being the second, *Vltava* (the river on which Prague stands).

More widely known to the outside world was a composer twenty years younger who played for some years in the Opera House orchestra under Smetana – DVOŘÁK. He had a wonderfully inventive mind, and there is a freshness and vigour about his melodies which is most enjoyable, whether they are lyrical or gay. At first he enjoyed a purely local reputation, but he was fortunate in attracting the attention of Brahms, who befriended him and interested his publishers in this 'very talented' composer, as he put it in his introduction. Dvořák's first great success came with the *Slavonic Dances*, in which he deliberately set out to write in the rhythms of his country's folk music. These lilting pieces carried his name all over Europe and to America. He visited England several times, where he became a great favourite, and later went to the U.S.A. for three years, where he wrote his most famous symphony (sub-titled *From the New World*) and other works. A new form which he introduced into music was the *Dumka*, consisting of a slow mournful movement with contrasting lively episodes. Dvořák's output was very large in almost every field, and it is worth remembering that in his case the opus numbers of his works are particularly misleading and bear very little relation to the order of composition.

There is so much delightful Dvořák that the choice for a beginning is very wide. You will find the Slavonic Dances great fun, and you can go on from them to his Slavonic Rhapsodies and thence to the 'Carnival' Overture and the symphonies (the 'New World' or the charming No. 4 in G major). A very lovely work is the Cello Concerto, of which Brahms said, 'Why didn't someone tell me it was possible to write a cello concerto like this? If I'd known, I'd have written one myself long ago!' Among his chamber music I would suggest trying either the Quartet in F (called the 'Nigger') or the 'Dumky' Piano Trio.

Contemporary with Dvořák in Bohemia, the amiable GRIEG in Norway was similarly building up a national style, although in his case he used more actual folk material instead of merely writing in folk style. He made his reputation with his striking Piano Concerto, which called forth high praise from Liszt, and which is still his most popular work. Allied to his treatment of folk music was a strong sense of classical form, but essentially Grieg was a miniaturist and far happier in small works. There is a distinctive flavour about his music, something peculiarly Norwegian, but he was apt sometimes to become too easily sentimental.

If you learn the piano you will probably come across many of Grieg's smaller piano pieces (such as the 'Lyric Suites'), which are very typical of the man; and you will get plenty of opportunities of hearing the Piano Concerto. You may already know his incidental music to 'Peer Gynt', and I recommend you to try the delightful 'Holberg Suite' for strings.

THE REVIVAL OF ENGLISH MUSIC

And what was happening in English music all this time? England was certainly not lacking in patriotic feeling, but, fortunately for us in other ways, we were not under foreign domination like Bohemia or Poland and so were not driven to express our national feelings in music as a sign of struggle. England had for so long welcomed foreign musicians, and had been so generous in her hospitality, that an over-modest tradition had grown up that visiting musicians from abroad must be better than our own musicians. In the eighteenth century Handel and his style had been all the rage; in early Victorian times, Mendelssohn with his suave elegance carried all before him; and after him nearly all the leading Continental composers were admired and welcomed here, even alarming revolutionaries like Wagner. So self-effacing were we that in the nineteenth century a performer had to have, or to take, a foreign name before the general public would believe he could be any good!

This silly attitude, springing originally from excessive modesty and good nature, was allowed to continue for so long that certain arrogant German critics sneeringly called us 'the land without music', and implied that all our music and musicians had to be imported. We are now gently having to blow our own trumpets a little, so that this myth can be disposed of for ever. (Unfortunately, in our genuine thirst for music and our interest in the best standards of performance, we are still welcoming large numbers of foreign artists, some of them admittedly of the front rank, but others no better than the general run of our own musicians, thus helping to bring about a continuation of the same situation.)

The lead in the revival of English music really came from two men, PARRY and STANFORD (who was an Irishman!), though of course there were others who also helped. Like Glinka, these two are more important as influences than as composers. Both had a sensitive feeling for the rhythms of poetry and speech, and thus were at their best in vocal music: Stanford specialized in songs and operas, and Parry's *Jerusalem* is practically a second national anthem. Both were fine teachers (Parry was Professor of Music at Oxford University, Stanford at Cambridge). Parry was a more 'county' type than Stanford, who combined a caustic wit with his breezy Irish manner, and this difference can be seen in their songs. The best of their choral works to be heard to-day are Parry's *Blest Pair of Sirens* and Stanford's *The Revenge* and *Songs of the Fleet*. Parry and Stanford paved the way for the next generation of composers, in which England was to show her musical strength; but the next figure to take the stage was a practically self-taught musician who was to make a great name for himself and for English music. As his career takes us into the present century, however, we will let him begin the next chapter for us.

9

The Men Who Wrote the Music: Part Three

IN 1901 an oratorio by an English composer which had been a comparative failure at its first performance the previous year in Birmingham was given a tremendous reception in Germany: so great in fact that it had to be repeated a few months later, when the Press hailed the composer as 'one of the leaders of modern musical art', and the foremost composer in Germany, Richard Strauss, proposed a toast to the success of the 'first English progressive musician'. The oratorio was *The Dream of Gerontius*, and the composer was ELGAR, who with this work struck a great blow for English musical prestige.

Elgar's career reads like a real success story. He received practically no tuition in music, and for some time had to earn his living as an orchestral violinist in the provinces. Very gradually, he managed to get some of his works performed, and worked up quite a reputation as a writer of cantatas for festivals. With the production of the *'Enigma' Variations* for orchestra and the success of *Gerontius* a year or so later he sprang to the fore. All kinds of honours were bestowed upon him in the years following, and he ended his life as Master of the King's Musick and as one of the most eminent figures in the European scene. His music, richly emotional and dignified, is the perfect reflection of the solid and assured prosperity of the Edwardian age in which he made his name. It is characteristic of him that his favourite stage-direction in his works is *nobilmente* – 'nobly'.

You are most likely to meet Elgar as an orchestral writer, though his cantatas and oratorios also have a considerable following. His 'Pomp and Circumstance' Marches (especially the one which contains the tune known as 'Land of Hope and Glory') show his command of broad flowing melodies, but they lack the delicacy to be heard in, for example, the 'Wand of Youth' Suites. You should certainly hear the 'Enigma' Variations, his masterly 'Introduction and Allegro' for string orchestra, and the very beautiful Cello Concerto which will be, I think, easier to grasp than the lovely but rather long Violin Concerto.

THE SYMPHONIC POEM AGAIN

Many of Elgar's orchestral works are programme music, among them the great symphonic poem *Falstaff*. It is interesting that his most famous contemporary, that same Richard STRAUSS I mentioned just before (whose orchestral style is not unlike Elgar's in texture), was the greatest master of the symphonic poem of modern times. He greatly admired the work of Berlioz and Liszt, and his own compositions carried their ideas much further in their virtuoso use of the orchestra, the expression of humour, and the representation of characters and even of natural sounds and events. There are, for instance, astonishingly realistic musical pictures in *Don Quixote* of a flock of bleating sheep and of the hero attacking the windmills. But the *artistic* value of these technically brilliant passages is not particularly great. Far more subtle are the musical portraits in *Don Juan*, *A Hero's Life*, or *Till Eulenspiegel* (the merry rogue of medieval times who after many adventures comes to a bad end).

Strauss made unheard-of demands on orchestral players' technique, writing complicated passages which were at first frankly declared impossible, and using in most of his works a very large number of instruments, including some strange new percussion effects. In later years Strauss simplified his style considerably, and wrote smaller works, such as the

Oboe Concerto, which are more sober than the fiery works of his youth. He also wrote a large number of operas, of which the best-known, combining the opulent chromatic harmonies of the post-Wagner period with colourful stage action and with gay waltz rhythms, is the comedy *Der Rosenkavalier* (*The Rose-bearer*). By the way, Richard Strauss was no relation of the two Johann Strausses mentioned earlier, and must not be confused with these composers of light music. As a well-known rhyme puts it:

> Johann Strauss
> Composed *Die Fledermaus*
> But Richard wrote properer
> Opera.

The most frequently played work of Strauss is the tone-poem 'Till Eulenspiegel', which is a good example of his brilliant orchestration. Apart from that, you would enjoy the suite of waltzes from 'The Rose-bearer', and there are several attractive lieder, including the famous 'Serenade'.

Most of Strauss's tone-poems were written a few years before 1900. It was at much the same time that tone-poems began to come from the pen of SIBELIUS, in distant Finland, and shortly afterwards he began writing symphonies, of which there are now seven, a further one being, despite the eagerness of the musical world, withheld from publication at present. Sibelius's music is based entirely on the legends and the spirit of his native country. His work seems to suggest a northern land of vast forests and lakes and of bitter winds. He is indeed one of the great nationalist composers. Not only do his tone-poems illustrate Finnish legends – *The Swan of Tuonela, Lemminkainen's Return, Tapiola* are examples – but there is a bleakness, a remoteness of thought, and a strange conciseness of language about all his work (including the symphonies) which is unique in music, and which obviously is the product of a mind which has preferred to keep apart from normal paths. His technique, both of form and of orchestration, is highly original, but he has no leanings towards extravagant resources, and if Strauss's music can be likened to a draught of heady and potent wine, Sibelius himself has said that his music is like pure cold water.

> *Sibelius's music is apt to be a bit puzzling at first because of his originality, and because, having said exactly what he wants to, he then stops abruptly. The Second Symphony is perhaps the easiest big work to start on; it is full of fine tunes and is at the same time most ingeniously constructed. Then I would recommend the haunting, melancholy 'Swan of Tuonela', and after that the symphonic poem called 'En Saga'. It is worth listening two or three times to Sibelius's works even if they don't appeal to you right away — you will find they grow on you.*

A NEW DEPARTURE IN FRANCE

Around the turn of the century a quite new style was being formed in France by DEBUSSY, who rebelled against accepted ideas of form and of harmony. His music was the counterpart of the 'impressionist' painting and the 'symbolist' poetry of his day, and he sought to escape from clearly-defined melodic phrases and firm key-feeling by using purposely vague and ambiguous chords, unfamiliar scale-systems and kaleidoscopic melodic patterns to produce a subtle, intangible, poetic kind of music as mysterious and fascinating as the shimmering colours of shot silk. In his youth, Debussy was befriended by the same rich widow who was financing Tchaikovsky, and with her he visited Russia, where he came into contact with the music of the nationalists. Ten years later he was much influenced by the Javanese players who, with their exotic instruments and music, were so great an attraction at the Paris Exhibition of 1889. His numerous piano pieces and his orchestral music, originally regarded as incomprehensible and shapeless, are now firmly established in the repertoire.

It is difficult to suggest a starting point for Debussy, for his is the kind of music that needs thought and imagination for its appreciation; but try some of the popular piano pieces first, like 'Clair de lune' or 'The Submerged Cathedral' or 'Minstrels' before you tackle the orchestral 'Fêtes' or 'L'Après-midi d'un Faune'. When you think you have the 'feel' of Debussy, you should try to hear his wonderful String Quartet.

In many people's minds the name of Debussy is often linked with that of RAVEL, thirteen years his junior, in rather the same way that Bach and Handel are often considered inseparable. Ravel, however, though he owed much to Debussy's harmonic experiments and shared a similar love of delicate effects, was of a totally different nature. As an American critic has well put it: while Debussy turned towards impressionism, Ravel remained classical at heart, and if Debussy derived from Chopin, Ravel was in the line of descent from Liszt. Unlike Debussy, Ravel retained a feeling for key-centre, and his piano writing and his orchestral scoring are in the virtuoso class. A number of his orchestral, chamber, and instrumental works are played, but his masterpiece is probably his music written for the Diaghilev ballet *Daphnis and Chloe*.

Ravel's very early and popular 'Pavane for a dead Infanta' is a fair introduction to his rich harmonic style, but far better would be the 'Mother Goose' Suite (for either piano duet or orchestra). Piano pieces like the Sonatina or 'Jeux d'eau' are very typical and easy to follow. Then I should try the String Quartet and 'Daphnis and Chloe'. The much-played 'Bolero' is not a good work, but it admirably shows off Ravel's astonishing orchestral mastery.

SPAIN, ITALY, AND RUSSIA

The lure of Spain had caused several French composers, among them Debussy, Ravel, and the gay and witty CHAB-RIER, to follow the example of Glinka and Rimsky-Korsakov and write works in the Spanish idiom. It is worth noting that, unlike the 'stage Spanish' of the Russians, the French composers produced works whose style was praised as authentic by the Spaniards themselves. But Spain, which possesses a great wealth of colourful folk song and dance, was beginning, about 1900, to produce her own national composers. The first to attract attention was ALBENIZ, a brilliant pianist who had been a pupil of Liszt, and who in his wide concert-tours in North and South America and throughout Europe played his own compositions, which are full of Spanish flavour. He lived for a time both in London and Paris, and it was in these two capitals that his style made the greatest impression. You will probably know a tuneful little *Tango* of his, but among his important works the best are the set of piano pieces called *Iberia*, very difficult to play but very exciting to listen to.

A contemporary of Albeniz, and another fine pianist, was GRANADOS, whose delightful *Spanish Dances* are popular, and who wrote a set of piano pieces (called *Goyescas*) based on paintings by the Spanish artist Goya, which have a poetic grace and delicacy and a characteristically Spanish elegance. The best-known of the *Goyescas* is the one called *The Maiden and the Nightingale*.

More important than either of these two was another Spaniard slightly their junior, Manuel de FALLA. Although he made a special study of his native folk-music, he scarcely ever quoted actual folk themes, yet his compositions are entirely Spanish in feeling and atmosphere, creating a wonderful impression by using certain harmonic and rhythmic devices characteristic of Spanish national music. Unlike the others, Falla was essentially a writer for the orchestra, and he was at his best when writing for the theatre. It was about the time of the first world war that Falla began to make his name, with his opera *La Vida Breve* (*Life is Short*), the ballet *Love the Magician*, and a beautiful imaginative work for piano and orchestra called *Nights in the Gardens of Spain*. His big chance came, however, as it came to several other composers (among them Ravel and Stravinsky), from Diaghilev's famous Russian Ballet company. In 1919 his ballet *The Three-cornered Hat* was first produced in London, and the colour and animation of his music created a sensation.

We have not, in this rapid survey, paid much attention to composers who wrote only operas, except where extracts from their works are a regular feature of the concert repertoire, as in the cases of Verdi and Wagner. We must find room now for a few words about another such writer, the most famous opera-composer of recent times and the most popular with the general public – PUCCINI. The secrets of Puccini's success were his choice of everyday characters and situations, his uncanny sense of the theatre and his ability to create an atmosphere in a few vivid strokes. He wrote well both for the voice and for the orchestra, and, although he had none of the nobility of Verdi, he excelled at expressing emotions such as pathos, tenderness, and cruelty. He could wring the last drop of sentiment out of a situation, and his detractors have found fault with some of his 'tear-jerking' technical tricks. But there is no doubt of his effectiveness as a stage-writer, and you are certain to come across arias and duets from his operas *La Bohème*, *Tosca*, *Madame Butterfly*, and *Turandot*.

With the rise both of nationalism and of the feeling for everyday emotions and situations (called *verismo*) to be found in the operas of Puccini and others, the outlook of the Romantic composers seemed to be out of date, though a highly emotional kind of music lingered on for a time in several countries as a kind of after-glow of Wagnerism. There was, however, one isolated late Romantic who must be mentioned – RACHMANINOV. He was a fine pianist, perhaps the greatest of his day, and many of his best works are for his own instrument; but he was a conductor and composer as well, and there is a considerable amount of his orchestral music which is only now beginning to claim attention. In style he was not unlike Tchaikovsky in some respects, but he had a personality of his own, and his long flowing tunes (he was an outstanding melodist), his rich and passionate melancholy and his mastery of form were all highly individual.

A mere handful of Rachmaninov's works has unfortunately so pre-occupied the minds of the public that the rest of his output is neglected. His songs include some lovely specimens, but they are less sung than they deserve to be. Far and away his most popular work – and one of his most finished efforts – is the Second Piano Concerto: this, with its magnificent sweeping tunes, is as good an introduction to his music as any. The Preludes and other piano pieces are mostly easy and satisfying listening, and for Rachmaninov's mastery of technique at its best you should hear his 'Rhapsody on a theme of Paganini' for piano and orchestra.

NATIONALISM IN ENGLAND AND IN HUNGARY

Folk-song flourishes most in countries which are largely agricultural. In industrialized England it was rapidly dying out except among a few country folk. And so, in the early 1900's, a number of enthusiasts set out to collect and preserve the folk music of this country before it should be completely forgotten. As a result, an enormous amount of valuable material was rescued, but it was unfortunately no longer a living tradition. When the wave of nationalism hit England, therefore, composers who based their style on the characteristic scales and turns of phrase of English folk-song were regarded in some quarters as being artificially 'folky', yet so successfully was this style assimilated, refined, and practised by certain composers that there very soon grew up a school of 'typically English' writers in a pastoral style. The greatest of these (who is happily still with us as the Grand Old Man of English music) is VAUGHAN WILLIAMS. He researched not only into folk music but into the nearly forgotten Church composers of Tudor times, and out of these two styles forged an individual one of his own, which has had a strong influence on nearly all younger English musicians. He does not – except in some of his earlier works – *quote* folk or Tudor themes, but they form a background which has coloured all his writing. Vaughan Williams has written little instrumental or chamber music, but is at his best in writing for chorus or for orchestra.

After sampling some of Vaughan Williams's folk-song arrangements such as the orchestral 'Folk-song Suite' or the choral 'Fantasia on Christmas Carols', listen to his re-creation of the spirit of Tudor England in his 'Fantasia on Greensleeves' or the solemn and wonderful 'Fantasia on a Theme by Tallis'. Then try some of his songs – the popular 'Linden Lea' and the 'Songs of Travel' would be a good choice – before starting on his more mature music – the song-cycle 'On Wenlock Edge', the 'London' Symphony (the second of his seven), and the beautiful 'Serenade to Music' for chorus and orchestra.

A great friend of his, though a very different kind of person, was his contemporary HOLST, who was for some years an orchestral player before devoting himself to teaching and composition. Although he had also helped to collect folk songs and had made many admirable arrangements, his style was not coloured by them in the same way: his thoughts were turned more towards Eastern mysticism. The bulk of his music is for chorus and for orchestra: he excelled equally with a large orchestra (as in the suite *The Planets* or the ballet music to his opera *The Perfect Fool*) and with a small one (as in his chamber operas or the very English *St Paul's Suite* for strings). His masterpieces are *The Planets* and the choral *Hymn of Jesus*.

Before either Holst or Vaughan Williams got under way, however, there was another composer writing essentially English music, although he lived most of his life in France, was greatly influenced by the music of his friend Grieg, and first received serious consideration in Germany! This was DELIUS. He was largely self-taught, avoided human society as far as possible, and for the last ten years of his life, although both paralysed and blind, managed to go on composing by means of the services of a devoted helper. Delius's music, which is the complete musical reflection of the English countryside and of poets like Keats and Shelley, seems at first to have little shape, rhythmic variety, or melody. Yet so powerful and individual is his (very chromatic) harmonic sense that he seems to wrap us in a subtle imaginative spell in which time ceases to exist.

The dreamy quality of Delius's imagination is apparent at once in his 'On Hearing the First Cuckoo in Spring' and even in the tiny Serenade from his music to the play 'Hassan'. The popular dance called 'La Calinda' from one of his operas is less characteristic. There are several beautiful songs, but the best Delius is in such orchestral works as 'Brigg Fair' (based on a Lincolnshire folk-song) or 'The Walk to the Paradise Garden' (an interlude from another opera).

While we are on the subject of English musicians, there are two other composers who should be mentioned. The first is BAX, dreamy, complex in style, and much influenced by

Irish legends and mysticism. His most popular works, apart from his songs and short piano pieces, are the brilliant orchestral Nature tone-poems *Tintagel* and *The Garden of Fand*. Slightly apart from the others because he has no folk-music background, but nevertheless typically English, is John IRELAND, a serious-minded though warm-blooded writer who has written many songs and piano pieces, and whose Piano Concerto and *London Overture* are frequently played.

This chapter would be less complete even than it is bound to be without a word on the two most important composers of modern Hungary – BARTÓK and KODÁLY. Like Holst and Vaughan Williams in England, they started off by collecting and studying their native folk music, and their styles are saturated with its flavour. You will not hear much of Bartók's rather intellectual chamber and orchestral music, but Kodály, a more approachable writer, is well known here for his folk-style *Dances of Galanta* and, still more, for the amusing and brightly-coloured suite from his opera *Háry János* (which nobody could fail to enjoy).

LIVING RUSSIAN COMPOSERS

Around the time of the first world war, certain composers in Europe were beginning to feel that everything in music had already been said, and that if the art were to progress further its vocabulary would have to be enlarged. Teachers and composers started to work out new theories, making all kinds of experiments with the materials of music. It is not our purpose here to try to follow (even if we could) the many new theories of art which have been proposed and tried. We are concerned only with leading writers. But our next composer, STRAVINSKY, sums up in his own work most of the experiments in the air at that time and since.

This pupil of Rimsky-Korsakov derived from his master a feeling for virtuoso orchestration as well as an intensely Russian style, although since the Russian Revolution he has never returned to his native land, living first in Paris and then in America. No one composer has had a greater influence on his contemporaries, and even if there is something in his opponents' accusation that he changes his style as constantly as a dress-designer changes his fashions, there is no doubt that he has always been a leader of any fashion he has chosen to set.

Stravinsky's great chance came with Diaghilev's Russian Ballet, for which his first work was the colourful *Firebird*. His next ballet the following year (1911), *Petrouchka* – a story of a puppet with human emotions – is perhaps his masterpiece: it created a great stir, and was an immense success. In this work were many experimental features, but it was his third ballet, *The Rite of Spring*, which seemed to the musical world a completely wild challenge to tradition. This work made bold experiments not only in orchestral technique but in tonality (no key-system at all or several simultaneous keys), in irregular rhythms, in harmony, and in melodic patterns. (It is typical of the speed at which music develops that this music, originally so shocking, is now quite at home in the concert repertoire.) In Stravinsky's later works he has written for curious combinations of instruments, for extremely small groups, in austere and deliberately non-expressive styles, and in a host of puzzling ways, but his later works are chiefly for the specialist audience.

Stravinsky's most important Russian contemporary was PROKOFIEV, who also wrote ballet music for Diaghilev, and who also worked in Paris and America, but later returned to the Soviet Union. Prokofiev's inclinations were towards the angular, the satirical and the grotesque, and most of his music, which is more tonal (that is to say, more in a key) than Stravinsky's, is rhythmically vital, almost heartlessly gay, and possesses a quality of mockery. Undoubtedly his easiest works to listen to are the *Classical Symphony* (in an elegant kind of mock-Mozart style) and the children's tale *Peter and the Wolf* for narrator and orchestra. But more typical, without being at all difficult to follow, are the March and Scherzo from his opera *The Love for Three Oranges* and the fairly frequently played Third Piano Concerto.

Two younger living Soviet composers whose names crop up in programmes deserve a word here. They are the Armenian KHATCHATURYAN, at his best in sparkling orchestration (as in the Piano Concerto and Violin Concerto), but whose music tends to be light-weight and sometimes (as in the ballet *Gayaneh*) just vulgar, and SHOSTAKOVITCH, a serious symphonist (he has written nine symphonies so far) who is known here mostly by his Concerto for Piano and Trumpet and by his youthful First Symphony. If some of his later works get a mixed reception here, it is partly because in Russia government officials lay down the styles in which composers shall write, and any offenders are severely dealt with. This artistic dictatorship – unthinkable in civilized Europe – is part of the price Russian composers pay for being supported by the State instead of, as elsewhere, having complete artistic freedom but having to struggle to make their own way.

LIVING COMPOSERS IN FRANCE AND ENGLAND

The mocking spirit of Prokofiev – a reaction against the sometimes excessive sentiment of the Romantic, and the solemnity of the Wagnerian, schools, and against the vague impressionism of Debussy – was also mirrored in France, where in the 1920's a group of composers known as *Les Six* proclaimed their faith in flippancy and a gay, jazzy, 'music-hall' style. This was little more than a passing phase, the musical equivalent of the foolish fashionable Bright Young Things of the day, but two composers at least of this group are worth notice here. One, more serious-minded than the rest, is HONEGGER, who attracted a good deal of attention with his programme music such as his impression of a railway train, *Pacific 231*, but who is to be heard at his best in his powerful oratorio *King David*, and the very original dramatic cantata *Joan of Arc at the Stake*. (Your best introduction to his music would probably be through the charming *Summer Pastoral* for small orchestra.) The other composer, better known though probably less significant, is POULENC, an irrepressibly witty writer whose songs and piano pieces are fair indications of his bright but miniature style.

The leading composer in England whose age corresponds to Poulenc's is William WALTON, certainly one of the finest creative talents in Europe. He can be witty, as you can hear in his early satirical suites called *Façade*, or the overture *Portsmouth Point* (full of rhythmic vitality and joviality), but it is his serious works which have placed him in the very front rank. Although dissonant, his music is not hard to follow because it does not merely strive after effect, it nearly always has a firm key-centre, it always possesses real melodies and it is superbly planned.

You will probably start on Walton with 'Façade' and 'Portsmouth Point' — and very invigorating they are — and with his film music (to 'Hamlet', 'Henry V' and others.) But I think you would find the lyrical Viola Concerto extremely moving, and if you want something wildly exciting you should hear his oratorio 'Belshazzar's Feast', in which he handles large choral and orchestral forces with gripping effect.

Finally, two younger composers: Alan RAWSTHORNE, one of the most thoughtful and serious minds in English music – he has written chamber works as well as some impressive orchestral music; and Benjamin BRITTEN, whose astonishing technical skill is evident in all his large output. You should certainly hear his music for the film *The Young Person's Guide to the Orchestra*, consisting of a set of variations on a theme of Purcell, and, as an example of his excellent sense of the theatre, the interludes to his most successful opera *Peter Grimes*.

A FINAL WORD

I hope I need not stress again that in these last three chapters I have been able to do no more than pick out some of the most important names in the history of music, and I am well aware that much more could be said even about the people I have mentioned. But my chief hope is that, when you see a composer's name in a programme, you will be able to get some idea of who and what he was (or is) and of his contribution to the ever-growing art of music. I hope, too, that if you come across a name we have not met here, you will have the curiosity to try to find out something about him, so that you can judge where he belongs. 'Does it really matter?', you may ask; 'can't I enjoy music without knowing who the composer was?' Well, yes, you can; but this historical sense is a very useful thing to have, for, although it cannot help you immediately to *enjoy* music any more, it can help you to *understand* it far better. And listening to music is a strange process in which we use both our emotions (for sheer enjoyment) and our brains (for understanding) together – but here we'd better start another chapter.

10

Listening to Music Intelligently

I CAN'T call this chapter 'How to enjoy music' because, strictly speaking, nothing anyone can say can increase your enjoyment of the sound of music, any more than it can increase your enjoyment of the sight of the sun shining, or the feel of crisp new snow. Either music appeals to you and gives you pleasure, or it doesn't; and if you get no pleasure from listening to the sheer sound of music, it won't be much consolation to understand how it is constructed and to know what to listen for – and you probably won't be reading this book anyway! The first essential of music is that it shall strike some responsive chord within us, so that we find we like it.

However, if we confine ourselves to letting the music flow over us like a pleasurable warm bath, we shall be like the kind of silly girl who comes out of a cinema saying that it was a *lovely* film, and who can tell you what pretty clothes the heroine wore, but who can't remember what the story was all about. In other words, music must be listened to not only with our emotions but with our brains; it must appeal not only to our instincts but to our minds; or, if you like, we should aim at understanding as well as enjoying it.

Listening to music is a complicated activity, and both feeling and understanding are necessary to get the best out of it. Knowledge without feeling produces merely a dry-as-dust pedant for whom (though he may not realize it) music will remain a closed book. Feeling alone, as I said, produces the person who 'doesn't know anything about music but knows what he likes'. Appreciation is something which can be increased by help and advice from other people, and you will find that you actually enjoy things more when you understand them too. Otherwise, after a few repetitions of even the most attractive piece, you begin to get tired of it, whereas with this double way of listening you can go on hearing a fine work again and again, discovering new interest in it each time.

GETTING READY TO LISTEN

There is one particular in which music differs from the arts of painting, sculpture, architecture, or poetry; it is that in music a question of time is involved. You can read a poem as slowly as you like, lingering over parts which attract you and going back as often as you want. You can stand and stare at a painting, a piece of sculpture or a building as long as you wish. But music, although it is written down and can to some extent be read like a book, really lives only in performance, and willy-nilly you have to go at its own pace. Once a sound is produced, once a passage is over, you cannot go back, but must make your thoughts follow what is happening all the time. That is why it is necessary to concentrate. If you let your thoughts wander during the performance, you may lose a vital part of the argument, as if at the cinema you had lost the middle of a film which was not going to be shown again. All this means that, if you are to get the best out of any music, you must be prepared to *listen* to it and not merely to *hear* it. In the concert hall, there are so many distractions – the sight of the orchestra and the conductor, the people round you, the printed words on the programme – that it is only too easy to let your mind wander. Once you do that, you're lost.

Now, long before you get to the concert, you can help yourself to listen. You will, I hope, have found out already

what is on the programme and something about the works
and the composers represented. The next step is to prepare
for the actual sound of the work. Intelligent listening to
music partly means trying to seize and understand the
design of the work as it flashes by, and there is a better
chance of doing this if you know beforehand from what units
the whole is built up. (If you saw the window-frames and
doors of an unbuilt house stacked up, you could tell at once
whether they were for a doll's house, a pre-fab, or a castle.)
So, with the musical works you are going to prepare for, try
to find out beforehand what the themes are; then you will
be able far more easily to appreciate what the composer is
doing with them and to see how the work hangs together.
Better still, get hold of a piano-duet version of the work (a
very large amount of music is available in this convenient
form) and play it through with someone beforehand. This
is good fun, anyway, and by actually making music yourself you can appreciate it far more in performance. With
a piano-duet arrangement (which of course you can go over
as often as you like, and in which you can repeat bits) you
not only get the hang of things far more readily, but, seeing
the notes before your eye as well as hearing them, you will
find they stay in your memory far better. But, however well
you play a piece of music, you will find it sounds different
when played by an orchestra – it is like the difference
between a drawing in black-and-white and a painting. Having become familiar with the black-and-white version,
however, you will not now be so dazzled, if the orchestral
colours are bright, that you can't tee what it is all about.

USING A SCORE

Undoubtedly the best way to get to know the music is
through the orchestral score. Miniature editions of what the

conductor has on his desk are not expensive to buy, they exist for a very large number of works, and they are of immense value to people who want to understand and appreciate music. You should try the experiment of playing through a piano-duet version of, say, a Haydn symphony, and then listening to an orchestral performance of the same work with a score in your hand. This seems to bring the music right into focus, and the fascinating glimpse it gives you of the wheels going round adds appreciably to the pleasure you get from the sound of the music. If you're trying your hand at it for the first time, don't be put out if you find you get lost. Your eye has to keep popping about from part to part to follow the themes, but a good plan is to concentrate largely on the first-violin line – a glance at the illustration on page 25 will show you that the strings are at the foot of the page – and occasionally to glance upwards to the woodwind, brass, and percussion and downwards to the rest of the strings. The main thing is at all costs not to get left behind; music, like time and tide, waits for no man. And don't forget, in the excitement of following, to keep your ears open as well as your eyes.

WAS IT A GOOD PERFORMANCE?

As you probably know, one of the most popular series of concerts in England is the annual series of Promenade Concerts (the 'Proms') held in London. Every year observers and critics lament the fact, that the audience, keen, enthusiastic music-lovers as they are, seem to be quite unable to distinguish between good, mediocre, and downright bad performances. When everything is equally applauded, critics rightly ask, 'Can this audience be said to have any musical understanding?' Recognizing the good and bad points of a performance demands expert knowledge, but there are certain things which you can decide for yourself fairly easily.

For instance, did you feel that the performers made the work interesting, or was it obviously a routine job for them? Was the rhythm of the work clear, or did it seem lifeless if slow, or scrambled if fast? In the case of an orchestral piece, were all the players exactly together in, say, a big chord, or did one or two come in just a fraction after the others? And could you hear everything that was going on, or was the tune obscured by other parts being too heavy?

In the case of a singer, could you hear the words? Did he pronounce them normally, or did he distort his vowels, clip his final consonants, or add what someone called 'boat-hook' endings (like a well-known singing film star who not so long ago cheered us with 'Hoome-a, hoome-a, sweet-a, sweet-a hoome-a')? Was his tone steady on long notes, or did he wobble? And did the singer appear to believe in the words – if the song was a sad one, for example, did he share its emotions, or was he too preoccupied with getting on good terms with the audience? Or, if it was a gay song, did he make you feel that gaiety, or was he rather half-hearted, giving the impression that it wasn't very good form to be amusing? (There is, by the way, an extraordinary reluctance on the part of some audiences to let themselves go. Where there is an obviously humorous passage in a work you can nearly always find people round you looking as solemn as judges. Some people appear to think that going to a concert is like going to church. Don't be afraid to find things amusing; very probably the composer meant you to do so. Not that you should laugh out loud, but if you think that something is funny by all means laugh to yourself – and afterwards tell someone about it and see if he or she thought the same.)

Some more questions: did the singer attack the notes

cleanly, or did he slither from one to the other all the time like a crooner or an old man singing in the street? Did he bellow out a top note just before the end in an effort to show you what a wonderful voice he had? Did he relax and treat the song as over as soon as he had finished singing, or did he regard the concluding bars in the accompaniment as a vital part of the song? Did he make you very conscious of his breathing? Did he split up the phrases according to the sense of the words or simply as his breath allowed (for example – 'I must go down to the seas again, for the call of the running tide' – *enormous breath* – 'is a loud call and a clear call', etc.)?

In the case of a pianist, was all his playing clear, or was it smudgy, over-pedalled, or uneven? Again, was there a strong sense of rhythm? And did he bang the piano unmercifully in the loud parts, or were his extremes of strength and of delicacy equally pleasing to the ear?

THE QUESTION OF STYLE

These, and many other questions on similar lines, you can usually answer for yourself, and they make quite a good basis for forming a judgement of your own. But there are other considerations which have to be taken into account that are more subtle and that need more detailed knowledge – questions of style. It's very hard to explain what style is, but speaking generally it can be said that many periods of time – and many individual composers – each have a very characteristic language of their own, and to attempt to play works of one period or of one composer as if they belonged to another is a bad fault. But how can this be done? you will want to know. Well, let us take one or two examples. We know that Bach's orchestra was, by modern standards, very small: to play his works with a full-sized symphony orchestra is to give the music false proportions. We know also that it is wrong to play Bach's keyboard music with too much 'expression' or gradations of tone (though not of course without any), because the keyboard technique of his day called, for the most part, for sudden changes from *piano* to *forte* without making gradual *crescendos* and *diminuendos*. We know that the maximum volume of sound which could be produced in the times of, say, Bach, Beethoven, and Richard Strauss differed greatly, and to play the *ff* of Bach at the Strauss level would again be a fault of style.

Or let us take the question of rhythm. The music of the Romantic period, and particularly that of Chopin, calls for a very free, flexible rhythm suitable to its wayward emotional and often almost improvisatory character. The technical term used is *tempo rubato* (literally 'robbed time'), and it means not keeping a strict rhythm but letting it fluctuate slightly according to the feeling of any particular phrase. You can see, however, that if every phrase were to be hurried or slowed down at will, there would remain in the piece as a whole no general feeling of tempo at all, so *rubato* may perhaps best be defined as rhythmic give-and-take. Now the music of Chopin positively demands this kind of treatment – we know from accounts of his playing that he himself used it – and, although Chopin left the *rubato* (which is too subtle to be written down) to the taste of the player, his music would sound all wrong without it. On the other hand, it would be equally wrong to use *rubato* in music dating from a period when it was unknown – in Mozart, for instance. (It is worth mentioning, in passing, that orchestral *rubato* is naturally harder to obtain, but that Elgar and a few other composers, by scattering directions liberally throughout their scores, have tried to achieve the same effect.)

One more word about style. You can see by now that we have to listen to works of different periods in different ways – that's why it helps so much to know something of the background of music. There are no two more dissimilar styles that we have to take in our stride than the *polyphonic* and the *homophonic*. These two words mean, respectively, contrapuntal writing, where the music is made up of various 'horizontal' strands of melody going on simultaneously and combining to produce the complete fabric, and harmonic writing, where one melodic line (not necessarily at the top) is accompanied 'vertically' by the other parts.

I mentioned in Chapter 4 the difficulty many people experience in trying to follow early music because of its unfamiliar polyphonic style. They attempt to listen to Bach's *Brandenburg Concertos* in the same way as to a Brahms symphony, and then complain that there's no tune in Bach. On the contrary, it would be true to say that there is far more tune in Bach than in Brahms, but instead of themes appearing one by one and being developed at length, they occur together, and a fragment of tune will be tossed about from part to part in imitation. So much is going on that it is too rich to take in all at once. In listening to contrapuntal music we have to take in the general effect as well as try to follow individual strands of the texture.

DID YOU AGREE WITH THE CRITICS?

I have suggested that you should train yourself in the course of time to form your own judgements of the performances you hear, and of course the same applies to the actual music. A very good idea is to keep a notebook for all your concert-going. Before you go, note down, if you can get them, the themes of the pieces you are about to hear, and then immediately after the concert jot down your impressions of the music and the performance. When next you hear the same work, you may be surprised at the change in your feelings towards it, but never mind if you think later that your first reactions were all wrong or even silly. This is the way in which everybody develops, and it shows that you are making progress in the art of appreciating music.

After you have been to a concert, you will probably find it very interesting to read what the professional critics say the next day, and compare it with your own impressions. All the better national papers have experts on their staff who are, mostly, reliable judges, but that doesn't mean that any critic's opinions are necessarily right. Indeed, critics often don't see eye to eye with each other; so that if you find your views and the critic's don't agree, be honest and stick to what you think, but remember that, with his greater experience and knowledge, his opinions are certainly worth very serious consideration. It's quite possible that you are right and he is mistaken – but the reverse is equally possible! You should realize that a work which is new to you, fresh and exciting, may to the critic be over-familiar and stale. You may know the story about the critic who had a nightmare and dreamed he was listening to Beethoven's Fifth Symphony, and then woke up to find he was! The critic can probably cast his mind back over so many performances of any one work that it will take an exceptional performance to rouse him to enthusiasm. To you, hearing the work for the first time, it may seem wonderful, but to him it may be very ordinary in comparison with what he has heard before.

It is this over-familiarity with the well-known that is responsible for something for which critics are often taken to task. People complain from time to time that the professional music critics concentrate too much on new or out-of-the-way music or on pet topics of their own. But imagine for

yourself the feelings of a luckless musician who has had to
sit down and write something new on a thousand-and-one
performances of Tchaikovsky's Piano Concerto. It's obvious
that to him the unfamiliar programme is far more interesting and gives him an opportunity of saying something fresh.
Besides, in these days the newspapers can spare very little
space for criticism, and there is a good deal in the theory
that a critic's duty is to say something about the new music
now being written and so help composers who are carrying
on the art of music, or about unfamiliar masterpieces of the
past which have a lesson for us to-day, rather than about
popular works which need no recommendation.

WHERE SHALL WE START?

So we come to a final question – where to start on the enormous repertoire of music? (How I envy those of you who
are just setting out on your adventures – what thrilling and
wonderful discoveries lie ahead of you! And they're no less
exciting because everybody has to make the same discoveries
all over again for himself.) There is so much to hear and so
much to choose from that you can equally well start in any
one of dozens of different periods or of different types of
music. It's rather like reading books: it's largely a matter of
what appeals to you from among what you first come across.
Having found something you like, try other works by the
same writer (the suggestions in Chapters 7–9 may help
here), then extend your range to works by composers a
little earlier or a little later, forming your own opinions as
you go and comparing your ideas with what you read. Give
nearly anything a chance: you may find that something you
don't much care for at first improves considerably on a
second hearing. After all, no one can hope to get everything
there is to be got out of any work at only one hearing. So

stick at it and hear as much as you can as often as you can. You will find that it is only poor music that won't stand repetition. The really great works can be heard over and over again with ever-increasing enjoyment.

Off you go, then, to your concert; and happy listening!

Some More Books To Read or Refer To

REFERENCE

Eric Blom: *Everyman's Dictionary of Music*, 1946. Very concise.

Percy Scholes: *Oxford Companion to Music*, 8th edition 1950. Full of information of all kinds.

Hubert Foss: *Concert-goer's Handbook*, 1946. Dictionary designed for casual reading too.

THE ORCHESTRA

Frank Howes: *Full Orchestra*, new edition 1950. All about the instruments.

Bernard Shore: *The Orchestra Speaks*, 1938. The orchestral player's point of view.

Gordon Jacob: *How to Read a Score*, 1944. An excellent guide.

J. Easson: *Book of Great Music*, 1931. An easy preparation for score-reading or concert-going.

CHAMBER MUSIC

A Hyatt King: *Chamber Music*, 1948. A very readable general introduction.

THE HISTORY OF MUSIC

H. C. Colles: *Growth of Music*, 2nd edition 1939. Very clear and understandable.

A. L. Bacharach (editor): *The Music Masters*, 4 volumes, 1948-1954.

ACCOMPANYING

Gerald Moore: *The Unashamed Accompanist*, 1944. Full of good sense and humour.

MISCELLANEOUS

Sir Percy Buck: *The Scope of Music*, 2nd edition 1927. Contains a first-rate chapter on how tunes are built.

Eric Blom (editor): *Music-lover's Miscellany*, 1935. A collection of interesting, strange, and amusing things that have been written about music.

Musical Terms

KEY TO PRONUNCIATION SYMBOLS

It is not always possible to write in English the equivalent of the exact sounds of foreign words. You should regard the pronunciations given here as a guide which will enable you to get reasonably close to the versions generally considered in this country to be correct, though they might sometimes sound a little different when pronounced by foreigners to whose language the words belong.

a as in bat
ā as in bate
à as in calm
ă as in aunt (pronounced *very* shortly)
e as in bet
ē as in beat
ė as in her

i as in bit
ī as in bite
o as in cot
ō as in coat
oo as in soot
ōō as in coo
oi as in boy
ow as in cow
u as in cut

ū as in cute
ü u with rounded lips as in French *lune*
aw as in fawn (very short)
g as in gold
ḡ as in the Scotch *loch*
an, on, in, un The French nasalized *n*

Other letters are pronounced as in English. If one syllable is to be stressed more than another, it is followed by ' (thus à'la). Two syllables that are to be slurred and pronounced almost as one are not separated by a hyphen; thus pyoo.

(I – Italian   G – German   F – French)

Adagio (a-dà'jyō) (I): Slow.

Affettuoso (a-fet-ōō-ō'sō) (I): Lovingly, with affection.

Alla (à'la) (I): In the style of

Alla marcia (màr'chyă) (I): In march style

Allegretto (al-lā-gret'tō) (I): Slightly less lively or quick than *Allegro*

Allegro (a-lā'grō) (I): Lively; but often used to mean merely quick

Andante (an-dan'tā) (I): At a gentle pace

Andantino (an-dan-tē'nō) (I): A little less slow than *Andante*

Assai (as-sī) (I): Very

A tempo (à tem'pō) (I): Up to speed

Ben (ben) (I): Well

Brio (brē'ō) (I): Vigour

Cantabile (kan-tá'bē-lā) (I):
With singing tone

Comodo (kǫ'mō-dō) (I): Convenient, comfortable

Con (kon) (I): With

Con fuoco (kon fwō'kō) (I): With fire

Con moto (kon mō'tō) (I): With a feeling of movement

Da Capo (dà ká'pō) (I): From the beginning

Dolce (dol'chà) (I): Sweet-ly

Giocoso (jyō-kō'sō) (I): Humorously

Grave (grà'vā) (I): Solemn

Grazioso (gràts-i-ō'sō) (I): Graceful

Langsam (lăng'zăm) (G): Slow

Larghetto (lár-get'tō) (I): Rather slow and solemn

Largo (lár'gō) (I): Slow, solemn

Lebhaft (lāb'hăft) (G): Lively

Leggiero (lej-yā'rō) (I): Light-ly

Lento (len'tō) (I): Slow

Maetoso (mī-stō'sō) (I): Majestic

Marcato (mar-kà'tō) (I): Well marked or accented

Mässig (mes'ik) (G): Moderate

Mässig bewegt (bė-vāgt) (G): At moderate speed

Meno (mā'nō) (I): Less

Meno mosso (mos'ō) (I): Less speed, slower

Molto (mol'tō) (I): Much, very

Mosso (mos'ō) (I): Motion, speed

Obbligato (ob-lē-gà'tō) (I): A part necessary to performance: sometimes, curiously enough, the exact opposite – a part for an extra instrument that can be added if desired

Più (pyoo) (I): More

Più mosso (mos'ō): More speed, quicker

Poco (pō'kō) (I): Little

Poco a poco (pō'kō á pō'kō): Little by little, gradually

Prestissimo (pres-tis'ē-mō) (I): Very quick

Presto (pres'tō) (I): Quick

Rasch (răsh) (G): Quick

Ruhig (rōō'ik) (G): Calm

Scherzando (skerts-ăn'dō) (I):
Scherzoso (skerts-ō'sō) } Playful

Schnell (shnel) (G): Quick

Segue (sā'gwā) (I): Follow straight on

Sehr (zār) (G): Very

Semplice (sem'plē-chā) (I): Simple, simply

Sempre (sem'prā) (I): Always

Senza (sen'tsa) (I): Without

Tempo (tem'pō) (I): Speed, pace

Tempo primo (prē'mō): At the original speed

Troppo (trop'ō) (I): Too much

Tutti (too'tē) (I): All; especially used for 'all the orchestra'

Vif (vēf) (F): Lively

Vivace (vi-và'chā) } (I):
Vivo (vē'vō) } Lively

Zart (tsărt) (G): Sweet-ly

TIME-CHART OF COMPOSERS

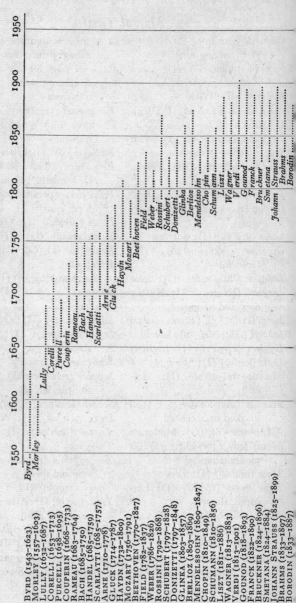

BYRD (1543–1623)
MORLEY (1557–1603)
LULLY (1632–1687)
CORELLI (1653–1713)
PURCELL (1658–1695)
COUPERIN (1668–1733)
RAMEAU (1683–1764)
BACH (1685–1750)
HANDEL (1685–1759)
SCARLATTI (1685–1757)
ARNE (1710–1778)
GLUCK (1714–1787)
HAYDN (1732–1809)
MOZART (1756–1791)
BEETHOVEN (1770–1827)
FIELD (1782–1837)
WEBER (1786–1826)
ROSSINI (1792–1868)
SCHUBERT (1797–1828)
DONIZETTI (1797–1848)
GLINKA (1803–1857)
BERLIOZ (1803–1869)
MENDELSSOHN (1809–1847)
CHOPIN (1810–1849)
SCHUMANN (1810–1856)
LISZT (1811–1886)
WAGNER (1813–1883)
VERDI (1813–1901)
GOUNOD (1818–1893)
FRANCK (1822–1890)
BRUCKNER (1824–1896)
SMETANA (1824–1884)
JOHANN STRAUSS (1825–1899)
BRAHMS (1833–1897)
BORODIN (1833–1887)

DVOŘÁK (1841–1904)
MASSENET (1842–1912)
GRIEG (1843–1907)
RIMSKY-KORSAKOV (1844–1908)
FAURÉ (1845–1924)
PARRY (1848–1918)
STANFORD (1852–1924)
ELGAR (1857–1934)
PUCCINI (1858–1924)
WOLF (1860–1903)
MAHLER (1860–1911)
ALBENIZ (1860–1909)
DEBUSSY (1862–1918)
DELIUS (1862–1934)
STRAUSS (1864–1949)
SIBELIUS (1865–
DUKAS (1865–1935)
VAUGHAN WILLIAMS (1872–
RACHMANINOV (1873–1943)
SCHÖNBERG (1874–1951)
HOLST (1874–1934)
RAVEL (1875–1937)
FALLA (1876–1946)
IRELAND (1879–
BLOCH (1880–
BARTÓK (1881–1945)
KODÁLY (1882–
STRAVINSKY (1882–
BAX (1883–1953)
PROKOFIEV (1891–1953)
HONEGGER (1892–
HINDEMITH (1895–
POULENC (1899–
WALTON (1902–
KHATCHATURYAN (1903–
RAWSTHORNE (1905–
SHOSTAKOVITCH (1906–
BRITTEN (1913–

Dvořák
Massenet
Grieg
Rimsky-Korsakov
Fauré
Parry
Stanford
Elgar
Puccini
Wolf
Mahler
Albeniz
Debussy
Delius
Strauss
Sibelius
Dukas
Vaughan Williams
Rachmaninov
Schönberg
Holst
Ravel
Falla
Ireland
Bloch
Bartók
Kodály
Stravinsky
Bax
Prokofiev
Honegger
Hindemith
Poulenc
Walton
Khatchaturyan
Rawsthorne
Shostakovitch
Britten

INDEX

For pronunciations, see key on page 176.
Page numbers in italics refer to the main entry.

LEWIS CARROLL'S

Alice's Adventures in Wonderland

AND

Through the Looking Glass

ARE NUMBERS PS35 AND PS44

IN PUFFIN STORY BOOKS

AND BOTH HAVE

JOHN TENNIEL'S ILLUSTRATIONS

2s each

KING ARTHUR

AND HIS KNIGHTS OF
THE ROUND TABLE

Roger Lancelyn Green

PS73

The King Arthur stories have here been told afresh from the original sources, vividly so that the simple plot emerges plainly and is exciting to follow through all the detail of feasting and jousting and the fearful impact of knights in armour. In it the old shape and purpose of the legends shines out, with Arthur's kingdom (the Realm of Logres) standing for right and chivalry against the barbarism which assailed it on all sides. Familiar names – London, Carlisle, Dover, and the Wirral – mingle with the magic ones of Camelot and Lyonesse, to remind the reader that the scene is laid, for the most part in these same islands of Britain. The many illustrations have been printed from pictures cut out of thin black paper by Lotte Reiniger. (2s 6d)

Family Afloat

AUBREY DE SELINCOURT

PS81

Elizabeth, Anne, father, mother, and Uncle Bob (soon called 'the Bosun') make up the pleasant family party which set out for a sailing holiday one summer in the *Tessa*, in spite of Daddy's gloomy forebodings that 'all sorts of things *might* happen'. But no one could have foreseen all that happened on that gay, eventful cruise. They sailed down the Channel almost as far as Brixham. They picked two Frenchmen out of the sea at dead of night. Half accidentally, they crossed to France – and that's enough to be going on with. You'll find out the rest when you read the book.

2s 6d

The Meeting-Pool

MERVYN SKIPPER

PS83

There is a sparkling freshness and humour in these tales of the animals of the Borneo jungle, who met every night at the drinking pool where no animal was permitted to kill. The animals were worried because the White Man was coming closer and closer to their haunts, chopping down the trees and burning them. These are the old folk tales of Borneo which in this telling keep their essential simplicity and salty humour. Sheila Hawkins has caught that humour deliciously in her animal pictures which illustrate it.

2s

A
PUFFIN BOOK OF
VERSE

Compiled by Eleanor Graham

PS72

This anthology is intended simply to give pleasure, and it is hoped that every boy or girl who browses among its pages will find something to enjoy.

It ranges from nursery rhymes and nonsense poems to verses whose meaning has to be thought about: but whether the poems are simple or more difficult, they have been chosen partly for that beauty of rhythm and language which makes lines linger in the mind long after the book that contains them has been put aside.

With decorations by Claudia Freedman

2s 6d